Field Guide
to the **Animals** of the
Greater Kruger Park

Christo Joub...
Ulrich Oberpri...
Burger Cilli...

GAME PARKS PUBLISHING

Niel Cillié

© Game Parks Publishing
P O Box 12331
Hatfield 0028
© Copyright of the 'Greater Kruger Park' map: Game Parks Publishing
ISBN 978-0-620385-48-0

Cover design by Steyn Pretorius

Map: REEB Advertising; Pretoria

Cover photographs:
Cheetah & Tree Agama – Niel Cillié
Roan Antelope & Little Bee-eater – Ulrich Oberprieler
Lion – Christo Joubert

Photograph on page 1: Lizeth Cillié

Illustrations by Anneliese Burger

Reproduction: Game Parks Publishing

Layout: NuDog Design, Pretoria, Tel: 012 342 2987

Printed by CTP Book Printers, Cape Town

First edition, first impression 2007
First edition, second impression 2009

CONTENTS

Introduction. 3
The Greater Kruger Park 4
Symbols 6
Mammals 8
Birds. 33
Reptiles and amphibians 111
Mammal Checklist 121
Bird Checklist 123
Acknowledgements & bibliography 130
Quick index. 131
Map 132

INTRODUCTION

The Greater Kruger Park comprises of South Africa's Kruger National Park, various private nature reserves to the west, as well as the Limpopo Transfrontier Park in Mozambique and Zimbabwe's Gonarezhou. Its 35 000 km^2 make up one of the largest conservation areas in the world.

It is situated in the so-called Lowveld, a wide coastal plain of relatively dry savanna that stretches from the Indian Ocean in the east to the escarpment in the west. Seven perennial rivers (the Crocodile, Sabie, Olifants, Letaba, Shingwedzi, Luvuvhu and Limpopo) transverse the Park. These rivers do not only provide life-giving water during the dry winters, but also support a subtropical riverine woodland along their banks. This unique habitat is utilised by a number of animal species that could not survive elsewhere in the Park.

The underlying geological formations and soils divide the Park into a further 15 ecozones, each supporting a unique vegetation type. This environmental mosaic is the main reason for the Park's large diversity of mammals, birds and other animals.

The Kruger National Park and the private nature reserves have a well-established tourism infrastructure. These vary from all-inclusive lodges to self-catering rest camps to picnic facilities for day-visitors. The Kruger National Park's 3000 km of roads, 23 rest camps, 11 picnic sites, three 4x4 routes, seven bird hides and six overnight trails offer an unequalled experience to the outdoor enthusiast. An infrastructure for tourists is gradually being developed in the Mozambique and Zimbabwean parks.

The aim of this book is to introduce the Park's unique and diverse animal life to its visitors, to assist them in the positive identification of the various species; thereby making their visit to the Park an interesting and satisfying experience.

THE GREATER KRUGER PARK

The 20 000 km² Kruger National Park in South Africa's north-eastern corner is surely one of the most well known and popular conservation areas in the world. More than one million visitors experience the park annually.

Paul Kruger, president of the then Zuid-Afrikaansche Republiek, voiced his desire to protect a part of the Lowveld from poaching and from being further divided into cattle farms. In 1898 the area between the Sabie and Crocodile rivers was proclaimed as the Sabie Game Reserve. After the Anglo-Boer War Col. James Stevenson-Hamilton was appointed as its first warden. His main duty was to curtail poaching, a task that he tackled with such enthusiasm that he was given the name Skukuza, meaning "The Man Who Sweeps Cleanly". In 1903 the Shingwedzi Game Reserve was proclaimed.

Stevenson-Hamilton's dream of a larger park became reality as in 1926 the Sabie and Shingwedzi Game Reserves were joined. Thus the Kruger National Park was born.

Danie Cillié (2)

Right: Skukuza 1950
Bottom: Letaba 1952

4

During the 1950's further rest camps were developed and Skukuza was extended. In 1959 a fence was erected around the park to prevent elephants and lions from entering commercial farms and communal lands. A few large mammals such as the rhinos and Lichtenstein's Hartebeest had become extinct by then, but were successfully re-introduced later.

The park's staff and scientists became well known for their expertise in wildlife management. Public opinion, however, turned against their policy of controlling the numbers of large herbivores such as elephants and buffaloes, and these programmes were stopped. Currently some surplus animals are relocated to other conservation areas, thus slowing overpopulation and the resultant negative impact on the habitat.

To create a larger ecological unit, the fences between the Kruger National Park and the private reserves along its western border were lifted in the 1990's. This initiated the concept of establishing an even larger unit across international boundaries, thereby re-establishing old migration routes of herbivores. A giant transfrontier park was thus created in 2002: the Greater Limpopo Transfrontier Park. This 35 000 km^2 park consists of South Africa's Kruger National Park, the Limpopo National Park in Mozambique and Zimbabwe's Gonarezhou. Together with the private nature reserves to the west this area is often referred to as the Greater Kruger Park.

This huge ecological unit is not only of benefit to its plants and animals, but also creates the opportunity for huge economic growth and poverty alleviation. The management of the park thus maintains the delicate balance between the needs of people and the need to conserve.

Translocation of White Rhinoceros

Lizeth Cillié

5

Symbols

The following easily recognised symbols are used to provide further information about the animals described in this book:

Habitat

Rest camps & gardens

Woodland & savanna

Rocky outcrops

Freshwater areas

Thickets

Mountain slopes

Grassland

Riverine woodland

Widespread

Food

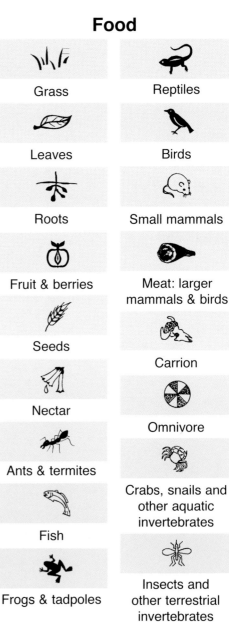

Grass

Leaves

Roots

Fruit & berries

Seeds

Nectar

Ants & termites

Fish

Frogs & tadpoles

Reptiles

Birds

Small mammals

Meat: larger mammals & birds

Carrion

Omnivore

Crabs, snails and other aquatic invertebrates

Insects and other terrestrial invertebrates

Active Period

 Day

 Night

 Dusk / dawn

Sociability (birds)

Solitary   Pairs

Family groups and small flocks   Large flocks

Symbols at photographs

Ad	**Adult**
Imm	**Immature**
Br	**Breeding**
NBr	**Non-Breeding**
♂	**Male**
♀	**Female**

Nest (birds)

The number of eggs laid is indicated

 Platform

 Cup

 Saucer / shallow bowl

Scrape in the ground

 Cavity in a tree

 Neatly woven nest

 Burrow in earth bank or in the ground

 Round or oval nest of plant material

NONE
UNIQUE
See text for description

EURASIA
Breeds elsewhere, not in the Park

BREEDING PARASITE
Uses the nest of a host

Migratory patterns (birds)

 Resident: Occurs throughout the year. Breeds in the Park.

 Summer resident: Present during spring and summer only, and breeds in the Park.

 Summer visitor: Present during spring and summer only, but breeds elsewhere.

The number next to the bird's scientific name is its Roberts' Number.

MAMMALS

Mammals are warm-blooded animals covered with hair or fur. The females produce milk to suckle their young. A number of mammals are large and thus easily seen by visitors to the Park. In addition, there is a far larger variety of smaller, mainly nocturnal mammals that are far less conspicuous.

Carnivores

Cats, wild dogs, jackals, hyaenas, otters, honey badgers, polecats, civets, genets and mongoose

Hoofed Mammals

All antelope, buffalo, Aardvark, pigs, zebra, giraffe, hippos, rhinos and elephants

Primates

Galago's (bushbabies), monkeys and baboons

Small Mammals

Squirrels, dormice, porcupine, hare, springhare, hyrax (dassies), bats, canerats, rats and mice

Carnivores

These animals belong to the mammalian order Carnivora. Although the majority of species are flesheaters, some (such as the Aardwolf) feed mainly on insects, while species such as the African Civet include berries, fruit and other plant material in their diet. All members of the Carnivora are predators, either specialised or opportunistic, and are characterised by their long canine teeth.

The various mongoose species show an interesting range of social behaviour: animals such as the Slender Mongoose are solitary, while Dwarf and Banded Mongoose have complex social interactions. The related African Civet and the genets are nocturnal and thus not often seen, neither are the otter, badger or polecat.

The social Spotted Hyaena is both a scavenger and an active predator. Brown Hyaena are less often seen, as they are shy scavengers usually foraging on their own. The Aardwolf is one of the most specialised mammals on earth, feeding primarily on harvester termites.

Jackals are quite opportunistic in their feeding habits, while the social African Wild Dog hunts in a cooperative fashion. The cats are probably the most specialised of all carnivores, as indicated by their strong bodies and short, powerful jaws. Most cats stalk and pounce onto their prey, but the Cheetah is a high-speed chaser.

White-tailed Mongoose
Ichneumia albicauda
Witstertmuishond

A large mongoose. The dark body contrasts with the whitish tail, which is large and fluffy. The long legs are almost black. This mainly solitary animal is only active from sunset until about midnight. During the day it rests in abandoned Aardvark or Springhare holes. It prefers moist savanna and grassland. It rarely climbs trees.

Jeanette Mathews

Length	Active Period
♂±110cm ♀±101cm	
Mass	
♂±4.5kg ♀±4.1kg	

±5.5cm

Habitat   Food

Marsh Mongoose
(Water Mongoose)
Atilax paludinosus
Watermuishond

This dark brown mongoose has a broad head. Long hair covers the body and tail. It is an excellent swimmer and will take to water when threatened. Mainly solitary, it is usually active at sunrise and sunset, using paths along the water's edge in search of food. Its diet consists of both aquatic and terrestrial prey.

Burger Cillié

Length	Active Period
♂±88cm ♀±85cm	
Mass	
♂±3.4kg ♀±3.4kg	

±6cm

Habitat   Food

Christo Joubert

Slender Mongoose
Galerella sanguinea
Swartkwasmuishond

The Slender Mongoose is reddish-brown with a long slender tail, which curves upwards towards the dark tip. The long tail and its larger size distinguish it from the similar Dwarf Mongoose. Mainly solitary and diurnal, it prefers open areas with sufficient shelter. It moves quickly and stands inquisitively on its hindlegs when disturbed.

Length	Active Period
♂± 60cm ♀± 56cm	
Mass	
♂± 5.3kg ♀± 4.7kg	

Habitat	Food

±3cm

Niel Cillié

Banded Mongoose
Mungos mungo
Gebande Muishond

These greyish-brown mongoose have characteristic dark, transverse bands on their backs. They live in cohesive groups and will usually unite in attack against enemies. The group communicates by continual twittering. They prefer areas with sufficient trees and undergrowth, usually close to streams, where logs and termite mounds serve as shelter.

Length	Active Period
♂± 54cm ♀± 54cm	
Mass	
♂± 1.3kg ♀± 1.4kg	

Habitat	Food

±3cm

Ulrich Oberprieler

Dwarf Mongoose
Helogale parvula
Dwergmuishond

This dark brown animal is the smallest mongoose in Southern Africa. It resem-bles a rat with a very thick tail. Gregarious. All members of the group help to raise the young. They communi-cate with "chook" sounds while foraging. They prefer dry, open woodland or savanna with sufficient shelter like fallen trees or termite mounds.

Length	Active Period
♂± 36cm ♀± 34cm	
Mass	
♂± 0.23kg ♀± 0.18kg	

Habitat	Food

±2.5cm

African Civet
Civettictis civetta
Afrika-siwet

The Civet is much larger than the genets. The body is whitish-grey with black spots and stripes. It has white blotches on either side of the nose and a black band across the eyes. It has acute senses and is exclusively nocturnal. Mainly solitary and very shy, it prefers areas with sufficient fruit-bearing plants and undergrowth that attract insects.

Length	Active
♂±129cm ♀±129cm	Period
Mass	
♂±10.9kg ♀±11.6kg	

Habitat

Food

 ±6cm

Anthony Bannister / Gallo Images

Small-spotted Genet
Genetta genetta
Kleinkolmuskejaatkat

This genet is easily confused with the Common Large-spotted Genet. The body, however, is a greyish colour with small black spots and the black-ringed tail ends in a characteristic white tip. It is exclusively nocturnal and solitary. It prefers open savanna, but occurs in various habitats from riverine trees to dry scrub.

Length	Active
♂±95cm ♀±92cm	Period
Mass	
♂±1.9kg ♀±1.9kg	

Habitat

Food

 ±3cm

Clem Haagner

Common Large-spotted Genet
Genetta maculata
Rooikolmuskejaatkat

Similar to the Small-spotted Genet, but it has larger, rusty-brown spots and the tail ends in a black tip. Although widely distributed, it is more common in the moister northern regions of the park. It prefers woodland and thickets along waterways. Nocturnal, shy and mainly solitary. Hunts both on the ground and in trees.

Length	Active
♂±91cm ♀±88cm	Period
Mass	
♂±1.9kg ♀±1.8kg	

Habitat

Food

 ±3cm

Lizeth Cillié

Ulrich Oberprieler

African Clawless Otter
Aonyx capensis
Groototter

Usually seen in or near water. The dark brown body and long thick tail as well as the white cheeks and throat are characteristic. This aquatic mammal has webbed hind feet for swimming. It uses its clawless front feet to search for and grasp food. It preys on frogs, crabs, reptiles and fish, which it takes head first. Mainly diurnal.

Length	Active
♂±118cm ♀±157cm	Period
Mass	
♂±12.3kg ♀±14.3kg	

Habitat	Food

±12.5cm

Burger Cillié

Honey Badger
Mellivora capensis
Ratel

The body is black with whitish-grey upperparts. The skin is loose and very tough. The short legs and large claws are used to dig for food. Omnivorous and fond of honey. Occur solitary or in pairs and mainly nocturnal. The Honey Badger is fearless and will attack even larger animals when threatened. Adaptable to various habitats.

Length	Active
♂±95cm ♀±95cm	Period
Mass	
♂±11.7kg ♀±11.5kg	

Habitat	Food

±8cm

SANParks

Striped Polecat
Ictonyx striatus
Stinkmuishond

The Striped Polecat has black and white bands of long hair on its back. There are three white patches on the face: one on the forehead and one below each ear. Usually solitary and nocturnal, it adapts easily to its environment, but is very scarce in Kruger. It will eject a foul-smelling fluid from the anal glands in self-defence.

Length	Active
♂±63cm ♀±60cm	Period
Mass	
♂±0.9kg ♀±0.7kg	

Habitat	Food

±3cm

Aardwolf
Proteles cristatus
Aardwolf

This jackal-like animal has a sloping back and a mane of long course hair. The black transverse stripes on the body and legs are characteristic. Nocturnal and solitary. It feeds almost exclusively on termites and can devour more than 250 000 termites each night. It prefers open areas like dry floodplains, but is scarce in Kruger.

Shoulder Height ♂±50cm ♀±50cm Mass ♂±8.9kg ♀±8.7kg	Active Period	±5.5cm
Habitat	Food	

Clem Haagner

Brown Hyaena
Parahyaena brunnea
Bruinhiëna

The body is covered with long brown hair, which distinguishes it from the more common Spotted Hyaena. The legs have pale brown rings. Nocturnal. Its exceptional sense of smell enables it to locate carrion several kilometres away. It forages alone, but is usually attached to a group within a fixed territory. Shy and retiring.

Shoulder Height ♂±79cm ♀±74cm Mass ♂±40kg ♀±38kg	Active Period	±8cm
Habitat	Food	

Clem Haagner

Spotted Hyaena
Crocuta crocuta
Gevlekte Hiëna

The dark spots distinguish it from the less common Brown Hyaena. A strict hierarchy exists amongst the sexes in a clan, with the heavier females dominant over the males. Very vocal, making giggling sounds in addition to the well-known "who-hoop" call at night. These scavengers are also successful hunters, catching even large antelope.

Shoulder Height ♂±80cm ♀±79cm Mass ♂±63kg ♀±68kg	Active Period	±10.5cm
Habitat	Food	

Burger Cillié

Lizeth Cillié

African Wild Dog
Lycaon pictus
Wildehond

A dog-like animal with characteristic large rounded ears. Each animal's coat has a unique pattern of yellow, white, black and brown blotches. The tip of the tail is always white. They hunt in packs of 10 to 15 animals. Back at the den they regurgitate some of the meat for the pups to eat. This is one of Africa's most endangered mammals.

Shoulder Height	Active Period
♂±68cm ♀±68cm	
Mass	
♂±28kg ♀±24kg	

Habitat | Food

±8cm

Burger Cillié

Side-striped Jackal
Canis adustus
Witkwasjakkals

Greyish-brown, with white stripes on the flanks. The white tail tip distinguishes it from the Black-backed Jackal. Territorial, with a long-term mated pair and their offspring occupying a territory. Its omnivorous behaviour, relying on fruit when other food is unavailable, helps it to adapt to the environment. It prefers moist woodland.

Shoulder Height	Active Period
♂±39cm ♀±39cm	
Mass	
♂±9.4kg ♀±8.3kg	

Habitat | Food

±5cm

Burger Cillié

Black-backed Jackal
Canis mesomelas
Rooijakkals

It differs from the Side-striped Jackal in that it is reddish-brown with a black-and-white "saddle" on the back. Omnivorous, but better known as a scavenger and as such it has a keen sense of smell. Also hunts various small animals. It prefers open areas and is mainly seen at dawn or dusk. Pairs are territorial but each jackal usually forages alone.

Shoulder Height	Active Period
♂±38cm ♀±38cm	
Mass	
♂±7.9kg ♀±6.6kg	

Habitat | Food

±6.5cm

Lion
Panthera leo
Leeu

Africa's largest cat, and the only one to live in prides. Well known and unmistakable. Young animals may have a slightly spotted coat. Predominantly nocturnal, lions usually sleep during the day. They prefer larger antelope such as Impala and Blue Wildebeest, but hunt a large variety of prey. White lions may be seen in the Timbavati area.

Shoulder Height	Active Period
♂±106cm ♀±91cm	
Mass	
♂±190kg ♀±126kg	

Habitat

Food

12.5 - 15.5cm

Christo Joubert

Leopard
Panthera pardus
Luiperd

The Leopard differs from the Cheetah in that it is sturdier and its spots are arranged in small clusters. Solitary and mainly nocturnal, but may be seen during the day. It usually drags its prey into a tree to prevent it from being stolen by other predators such as Spotted Hyaenas or Lions, and returns later to feed again.

Shoulder Height	Active Period
♂±68cm ♀±63cm	
Mass	
♂±63kg ♀±37kg	

Habitat

Food

9 - 10cm

Lizeth Cillié

Cheetah
Acinonyx jubatus
Jagluiperd

The single spots on the coat, "tear marks" on the face and slender body distinguish the Cheetah from the Leopard. The Cheetah is the fastest land mammal: it can reach a speed of up to 110 km/h over a short distance. It is usually solitary or in small groups and predominantly diurnal, as it needs to see its prey while sprinting.

Shoulder Height	Active Period
♂±87cm ♀±86cm	
Mass	
♂±54kg ♀±43kg	

Habitat

Food

8.5 - 11.5cm

Niel Cillié

15

SANParks

Caracal
Caracal caracal
Rooikat

A well-built, reddish-brown cat with large paws. The ears are distinctly tufted. Mainly nocturnal and solitary, it prefers open savanna and scrub, often near rocky outcrops. It lives and hunts mostly on the ground but may climb trees. It preys on small mammals, reptiles and birds; occasionally taking animals bigger than itself.

Shoulder Height
♂±43cm ♀±43cm
Mass
♂±13.8kg ♀±11.9kg

Active Period

Habitat

Food

 ±6cm

African Wild Cat
Felis silvestris lybica
Vaalboskat

Resembles the domestic "tabby" cat, but has longer legs. The back of the ears is distinctly rufous. The most common of Kruger's three small cat species, especially north of the Sabie River. Solitary and mainly nocturnal, but may be seen during the day. Forages predominantly on the ground. Cross-breeds with domestic cats.

Shoulder Height
♂±36cm ♀±34cm
Mass
♂±5.1kg ♀±4.2kg

Active Period

Habitat

Food

 ±3.5cm

Niel Cillié

Ulrich Oberprieler

Serval
Leptailurus serval
Tierboskat

A slender, long-legged cat with a short tail. The black stripes on the neck change into spots that cover the rest of the body. The large ears enable it to locate prey. The long legs are used to jump up and pounce onto prey. Nocturnal and usually solitary, it prefers grassy savannas and marshes with permanent water. Rarely seen.

Shoulder Height
♂±56cm ♀±56cm
Mass
♂±11.1kg ♀±9.7kg

Active Period

Habitat

Food

 ±5cm

Hoofed mammals

The hoofed mammals (ungulates) are primarily herbivorous, although a few, such as the pigs, may include some flesh in their diet. The hoof, which is equivalent to the human fingernail, protects the toes while walking or running. As most hoofed mammals are potential prey to predators, they show a variety of defensive strategies: large size (African Elephant, rhinos or African Buffalo), defensive weapons (Warthog, rhinos or African Buffalo), speed (most antelope), large herds (Blue Wildebeest, Impala or Plains Zebra), secretive behaviour (Bushbuck or duiker), camouflage (Kudu or Nyala), inaccessible habitat (Klipspringer or Hippo) and may even hide in underground shelters while sleeping (Warthog).

The ruminants, i.e. those species that have compound stomachs and chew the cud, are represented by the Giraffe, the African Buffalo and the various antelope. Two pigs occur in the Park: the diurnal, well-known Warthog and the nocturnal, secretive Bushpig. Both species of rhino are endangered, but are well protected in the Park. The Plains Zebra (or Burchell's Zebra as it used to be called) is the Park's only zebra.

In spite of their hoof-like appendages the Hippopotamus, African Elephant and Aardvark are not true ungulates. Strange as it may seem, recent research has indicated that Hippos are related to whales! The Aardvark is an unique African animal that feeds primarily on ants.

African Buffalo
Syncerus caffer
Afrika-buffel
Unmistakable: large, cattle-like animals. Bulls are heavier and have larger horns than cows. Breeding herds may consist of hundreds of individuals: bulls, cows and calves. Young bulls may form separate bachelor herds, while old bulls may gather in small herds or live on their own. Buffalo graze on tall, coarse grass and are dependent on water.

Burger Cillié (2)

Shoulder Height	Active Period
♂ ±170cm ♀ ±140cm	
Mass	
♂ ±785kg ♀ ±715kg	

12 - 15cm

Habitat | Food

Blue Wildebeest
Connochaetes taurinus
Blouwildebees
Similar to, but smaller and more slender than the African Buffalo. Both bulls and cows have horns, but those of the males are larger. They prefer grasslands or open savanna with short grass. Highly gregarious, they may gather in herds of hundreds of animals. Are sometimes seen together with Plains Zebra. Often migrate from summer to winter grounds.

Shoulder Height	Active Period
♂ ±147cm ♀ ±135cm	
Mass	
♂ ±250kg ♀ ±183kg	

±10cm

Habitat | Food

Niel Cillié

17

Hoofed mammals

Burger Cillié

Lichtenstein's Hartebeest
Alcelaphus lichtensteinii
Mofhartbees

It is distinguished from the Tsessebe by its pale tawny colour and lack of black patches on the upper legs. Viewed from the front, the horns appear to form a circle. Both sexes have horns, those of the bulls are thicker. Gregarious. It was reintroduced into the Kruger National Park in 1985 and is considered to be very rare.

Shoulder Height
♂±129cm ♀±124cm
Mass
♂±177kg ♀±166kg

Active Period

Habitat

Food

±8.5cm

Ulrich Oberprieler

Tsessebe
Damaliscus lunatus
Basterhartbees

Dark reddish-brown, with black patches on the upper legs, shoulders, buttocks and face. Both sexes have horns. These are wide apart at the base and have a characteristic V-shape. They are grazers and prefer open savanna with medium tall palatable grass. They usually occur in small herds and are uncommon in Kruger.

Shoulder Height
♂±126cm ♀±125cm
Mass
♂±140kg ♀±126kg

Active Period

Habitat

Food

±8cm

Burger Cillié
Niel Cillié

Impala
Aepyceros melampus
Rooibok

A very common, medium-sized, reddish-brown antelope with a white belly. Only rams have horns. Highly gregarious. Non-territorial rams gather in bachelor herds. The breeding herds of ewes and young animals are usually accompanied by a single territorial male, but may be joined by more than one adult ram outside the rutting season.

Shoulder Height
♂±90cm ♀±86cm
Mass
♂±55kg ♀±41kg

Active Period

Habitat

Food

4.5 - 5.0cm

Roan Antelope
Hippotragus equinus
Bastergemsbok

It is greyish-brown in colour, while the Sable Antelope is much darker. The dark facial pattern and the long ears are characteristic. Both sexes have horns, those of the bulls are thicker. Almost exclusively a grazer, it prefers medium to tall grass in lightly wooded savanna. Usually occurs in small herds, but is rarely seen.

Shoulder Height
♂±143cm ♀±138cm
Mass
♂±250kg ♀±240kg

Active Period

Habitat

Food

10.5 - 11cm

Ulrich Oberprieler

Sable Antelope
Hippotragus niger
Swartwitpens

Bulls are magnificent animals with their black, shiny bodies and white bellies. Cows and young animals are reddish-brown, although old cows may also be very dark. Cows have thinner horns than bulls. Sable live in herds of five to 25 animals and prefer woodland and savanna with medium to tall grass. A mature cow leads the herd.

Shoulder Height
♂±135cm ♀±130cm
Mass
♂230kg ♀±220kg

Active Period

Habitat

Food

8 - 10.2cm

♂

Burger Cillié

Lizeth Cillié

♀

Eland
Tragelaphus oryx
Eland

The Eland is the largest antelope in the region. Their colour is greyish-brown. Bulls have thicker horns and are larger than cows. Even adult bulls are spectacular jumpers despite their size. When eland walk, a characteristic clicking sound may be heard. Gregarious, but old bulls may be on their own. Seldom seen in Kruger.

Shoulder Height
♂±170cm ♀±150cm
Mass
♂±700kg ♀±460kg

Active Period

Habitat

Food

12.5 - 14cm

♂

Niel Cillié

♀

Burger Cillié

Burger Cillié

Kudu
Tragelaphus strepsiceros
Koedoe

A large, elegant antelope. Bulls are characterised by their impressive spiral shaped horns. Occur in a wide variety of habitats. As Kudu are primarily browsers they struggle to survive prolonged droughts when trees loose their leaves. Gregarious. Kudu are awesome jumpers, even bulls can clear fences of up to 2 metres.

Shoulder Height	Active
♂±150cm ♀±135cm	Period
Mass	
♂±221kg ♀±152kg	

Habitat	Food

6 - 9cm

Ulrich Oberprieler

Nyala
Tragelaphus angasii
Njala

Bulls may be confused with Kudu, but are darker, have long hair on the body and yellow "socks". Ewes again may be confused with Bushbuck, but are larger and have conspicuous white stripes on the body. Nyala live in small herds and browse during the cooler parts of the day. They prefer riverine vegetation and are more abundant in the north.

Shoulder Height	Active
♂±112cm ♀±97cm	Period
Mass	
♂±107kg ♀±62kg	

Habitat	Food

4.5 - 6cm

Burger Cillié (2)

Bushbuck
Tragelaphus scriptus
Bosbok

A medium-sized, reddish-brown antelope with white spots on the body and white patches at the base of the neck. Only the ram has horns. Shy and solitary the Bushbuck has keen senses and is aggressive towards predators. Prefers dense vegetation such as thickets and riverine growth, and is not territorial. Feeds mainly on leaves.

Shoulder Height	Active
♂±80cm ♀±70cm	Period
Mass	
♂±45kg ♀±30kg	

Habitat	Food

4 - 4.5cm

Waterbuck
Kobus ellipsiprymnus
Waterbok

A large antelope with long greyish-brown hair and a white circle around the tail. Only the bull has forward-curving horns. Waterbuck are found in open woodland with medium to tall grass. They are never far from water, especially during the dry winter months. They usually occur in small herds, but may be found in groups of 60 or more.

| Shoulder Height ♂±170cm ♀±130cm Mass ♂±260kg ♀±230kg | Active Period ☼ |
| Habitat | Food |

8 - 8.5cm

Burger Cillié

Ulrich Oberprieler

♂ ♀

Southern Reedbuck
Redunca arundinum
Rietbok

It is more yellow-brown and larger than the greyish Mountain Reedbuck. The shins of the front legs are black. Only the ram has horns. They live in monogamous pairs and are territorial, but may temporarily gather in small herds. Graze early in the morning and late in the afternoon. Prefer floodplains and marshes with reed beds.

| Shoulder Height ♂90cm ♀±80cm Mass ♂68kg ♀±49kg | Active Period ☼ ☾ |
| Habitat | Food |

5 - 6.5cm

Burger Cillié (2)

♂ ♀

Mountain Reedbuck
Redunca fulvorufula
Rooiribbok

It is smaller, more greyish-brown and has shorter horns (rams only) than the Southern Reedbuck. The neck is pale brown with a black spot below the ears. When running away it displays the white underside of the tail. It prefers mountain slopes and rocky hills (Berg-en-dal area), but is very rarely seen in Kruger. It occurs in small herds.

| Shoulder Height ♂±75cm ♀±73cm Mass ♂±31kg ♀±27kg | Active Period ☼ |
| Habitat | Food |

±4.5cm

Burger Cillié

Niel Cillié

♂ ♀

Red Duiker
Cephalophus natalensis
Rooiduiker

Smaller than the Common Duiker. The colour is deep chestnut-red with a tuft o long dark hair between the horns. Botl sexes have short, straight horns. Mostly a solitary animal, but may occur in smal groups. Inhabits thickets around rock hills in especially the Pretoriuskop area It is seldom seen due to its secretive and mainly nocturnal habits.

Shoulder Height
♂±43cm ♀±42cm
Mass
♂±13kg ♀±12kg

Active Period

Habitat

Food

3 - 3.5cm

Common Duiker
Sylvicapra grimmia
Gewone Duiker

The colour is grey-brown with a black stripe from the forehead to the nose and a tuft of long dark hair between the horns. Only the ram has horns Shy and solitary, sometimes in pairs. I prefers thickets, riverine forest and areas with sufficient undergrowth. Has a keer sense of smell and sight. Disappears into dense vegetation when disturbed.

Shoulder Height
♂±50cm ♀±52cm
Mass
♂±16kg ♀±17kg

Active Period

Habitat

Food

3 - 4cm

Klipspringer
Oreotragus oreotragus
Klipspringer

A small greyish-brown antelope with a grizzled appearance The pre-orbita glands show as conspicuous black spots in the inner corner of the eyes It is associated with rocky areas and is therefore a sure-footed rock climber The ewe is heavier than the ram and lacks horns. Usually seen in pairs or family groups.

Shoulder Height
♂±58cm ♀±58cm
Mass
♂±11kg ♀±13kg

Active Period

Habitat

Food

±2cm

Suni
Neotragus moschatus
Soenie

Kruger's smallest antelope. The colour is reddish-brown and the tail is dark with a white edge. The upper lip protrudes over the lower one. Only the ram has short horns. It feeds during the cooler parts of the day. Prefers dense deciduous thickets. Restricted to the Pafuri area, where it is very secretive and seldom seen.

| Shoulder Height ♂±37cm ♀±36cm | Active Period |
| Mass ♂±5.1kg ♀±5.5kg | |

| Habitat | Food |

Niel Cillié

±2cm

Steenbok
Raphicerus campestris
Steenbok

A small reddish-brown antelope with white underparts and large ears. Only the ram has short horns. May be confused with Sharpe's Grysbok. Pairs are territorial, but usually forage on their own. They are quite common and widely distributed, but prefer open grassy areas where there is adequate shelter in the form of tall grass and bushes.

| Shoulder Height ♂±52cm ♀±52cm | Active Period |
| Mass ♂±10.9kg ♀±11.3kg | |

| Habitat | Food |

Niel Cillié (2)

3 - 4cm

Sharpe's Grysbok
Raphicerus sharpei
Tropiese Grysbok

Differs from the Steenbok by the longer reddish-brown coat covered with white streaks. Only the ram has horns. Usually solitary or in pairs, this small antelope has a secretive nature and is seldom seen due to being essentially nocturnal. Grysbok prefer thickets or areas with shrubs. More common in the central and northern parts of the Park.

| Shoulder Height ♂±47cm ♀±47cm | Active Period |
| Mass ♂±7.3kg ♀±7.7kg | |

| Habitat | Food |

Burger Cillié

Niel Cillié

±2.5cm

23

Clem Haagner

Aardvark (Antbear)
Orycteropus afer
Erdvark

This solitary and nocturnal animal has an elongated, pig-like snout, long ears and a thick tapering tail. It has a very good sense of smell and hearing, but poor eyesight. An active and noisy digger that feeds on ants and termites. It prefers open woodland and grassland with soft soil and a large supply of ants. Is very rarely seen.

Shoulder Height
♂±61cm ♀±61cm
Mass
♂±53kg ♀±51kg

 Active Period

 Habitat Food

 ±11cm

Ulrich Oberprieler

Common Warthog
Phacochoerus africanus
Vlakvark

♀

Grey in colour, with little body hair, but may take on the colour of the soil after wallowing. The boar (male) has longer tusks and two pairs of warts on the face. The tail is held erect while running. Warthogs live in family groups. They utter grunting, growling and squealing sounds. Sleep in Aardvark dens or other hollows at night.

Shoulder Height
♂±68cm ♀±60cm
Mass
♂±80kg ♀±56kg

Active Period

Habitat Food

 3.5 - 4.5cm

Jeanette Mathews

Bushpig
Potamochoerus larvatus
Bosvark

The long brownish body hair and the mane of lighter hair on the shoulders distinguish them from Warthogs. They live in small groups in thickets and riverine vegetation, and are seldom seen. They are aggressive when there are piglets or when threatened. Nocturnal; during the day they rest in dense undergrowth.

Shoulder Height
♂±75cm ♀±70cm
Mass
♂±72kg ♀±68kg

Active Period

Habitat Food

 ±5cm

Plains Zebra
(Burchell's Zebra)
Equus quagga
Vlaktekwagga (Bontsebra)

This is the only zebra occurring in Kruger. The stripe pattern differs from one animal to another, and thus serves as an idividual "fingerprint" in the herd. Highly gregarious. Zebra are common throughout the Park, but prefer open grassland and plains. Often seen in association with Blue Wildebeest.

Shoulder Height	Active Period
♂±134cm ♀±134cm	
Mass	
♂±313kg ♀±302kg	

Habitat	Food

10.5 - 11.5cm

Christo Joubert

Giraffe
Giraffa camelopardalis
Kameelperd

Unmistakable with its long legs and neck. The brown patches on the male's body darken with age. Both sexes have short horns. Giraffes form herds, but individuals wander between herds. Bulls fight by standing next to each other and striking with their heads. Giraffes defend themselves by kicking with their heavy hooves.

Shoulder Height	Active Period
♂±330cm ♀±280cm	
Mass	
♂±1192kg ♀±828kg	

Habitat	Food

±19cm

Burger Cillié

Hippopotamus
Hippopotamus amphibius
Seekoei

Unmistakable barrel-shaped animals with short legs. Well-adapted to an aquatic life: the eyes, ears and nostrils are above the water level while the rest of the body is submerged. These nocturnal grazers use the same easily recognised network of footpaths: two parallel ruts with a central elevated strip. Aggressive towards intruders.

Shoulder Height	Active Period
♂±150cm ♀±144cm	
Mass	
♂±1546kg ♀±1385kg	

Habitat	Food

±24cm

Niel Cillié

Burger Cillié

African Savanna Elephant
Loxodonta africana
Afrika-olifant

Well known and unmistakable. Elephants live in herds: bulls-only bachelor herds and breeding herds of cows and youngsters with a mature cow as leader. Some older bulls wander alone. Elephants have a keen sense of hearing but poor eyesight. They are usually peaceful, but may be dangerous when protecting their calves.

Shoulder Height	Active Period
♂±350cm ♀±240cm	
Mass	
♂±5750kg ♀±3800kg	

Habitat   Food

 F

50 - 52cm

52 -

H

Ulrich Oberprieler

White Rhinoceros
Ceratotherium simum
Witrenoster

This rhinoceros is the second heaviest mammal in Kruger. In spite of its name, it is grey-brown in colour. The long head with a square-shaped mouth is well adapted for grazing. The head is normally held low. It prefers open savanna with thickets for cover. Males mark their territories with typical dung middens.

Shoulder Height	Active Period
♂±180cm ♀±177cm	
Mass	
♂±2200kg ♀±1600kg	

Habitat   Food

28 - 30cm

Ulrich Oberprieler

Black Rhinoceros
Diceros bicornis
Swartrenoster

It differs from the White Rhinoceros in the pointed upper lip and shorter head, which is normally carried higher off the ground. It is also smaller and more aggressive. Usually solitary. It has poor eyesight, but a keen sense of hearing and smell. A browser, it uses its pointed upper lip like a finger to pick off leaves. Secretive and rarely seen.

Shoulder Height	Active Period
♂±160cm ♀±160cm	
Mass	
♂±850kg ♀±880kg	

Habitat   Food

22 - 24cm

Primates

The Park's primates belong to two groups: the nocturnal galagos (bushbabies) and the diurnal monkeys and baboon.

The two galagos may easily be distinguished by size: the South African Galago is much smaller than the cat-sized Greater Galago. Both live in trees and are well known for their extraordinary jumping abilities. The huge eyes enable them to see at night, while the large ears indicate an acute sense of hearing. They feed on fruit, berries and insects, but include a large amount of gum in their diet, especially that of Acacia trees.

The intricate social behaviour within a troop of monkeys or baboons is usually worth watching. There is a strict order of dominance amongst individuals, with males dominant over females. Observe how individuals communicate with each other, not only vocally, but also by body stance and eye contact. Mutual grooming strengthens the bond within the troop. By playing with each other and older mates, young primates learn appropriate social behaviour.

Chacma Baboons and especially Vervet Monkeys easily become used to the presence of people. As they loose their sense of fear, they may become both a nuisance by stealing food and a serious danger by threatening children. Cute as they may be, wild primates should never be given food in

South African Galago
(Lesser Bushbaby)
Galago moholi
Suid-Afrikaanse Nagapie

The large ears, huge eyes and the long hind legs and tail characterise this small primate. It prefers mopane and acacia savanna. Gum is essential in its diet. It forages alone at night, but small groups rest together during the day. Takes huge leaps from tree to tree. Urinates on its hands and feet for scent-marking.

Length ♂±38cm ♀±36cm Mass ♂±0.16kg ♀±0.15kg	Active Period
Habitat	Food

 ±3cm

Niel Cillié

Greater Galago
(Thick-tailed Bushbaby)
Otolemur crassicaudatus
Bosnagaap

This galago is about the size of a small cat: much larger than the South African Galago. The fur, especially on the tail, is long and soft. Nocturnal, they forage alone but live in family groups. Urinate on their hands and feet. The loud, crying calls are often heard at night in suitable forest-like habitat.

Length ♂±74cm ♀±73cm Mass ♂±1.2kg ♀±1.1kg	Active Period
Habitat	Food

 ±4cm

Ulrich Oberprieler

27

Niel Cillié

Chacma Baboon
Papio hamadryas ursinus
Kaapse Bobbejaan
Unmistakable. Males are larger with long canine teeth and are more aggressive than females. Omnivorous. They forage during the day and sleep at night in tall trees or on cliffs. Baboons live in troops that vary in size from 15 to about 70 animals. A strict hierarchy of dominance exists within the troop. The loud bark of large males is often heard.

Shoulder Height	Active Period	
♂±71cm ♀±61cm		
Mass		
♂±36kg ♀±16kg		±8.5cm / ±15cm F / H

Habitat	Food

Niel Cillié

Vervet Monkey
Cercopithecus pygerythrus
Blouaap
Greyish-brown with a black face and long tail. Males are larger than females with a characteristic blue scrotum. Troops may vary in size, but have a distinct social hierarchy. At home on the ground and in trees. They become very tame and can become both a nuisance and a danger at rest camps and picnic spots where people feed them.

Shoulder Height	Active Period	
♂±31cm ♀±26cm		
Mass		
♂±5.5kg ♀±4.1kg		±8cm / ±9.5cm F / H

Habitat	Food

Niel Cillié (2)

Sykes' Monkey
(Samango Monkey)
Cercopithecus albogularis
Samango-aap
This monkey is restricted to the Pafuri/ Punda Maria area where it occurs in forest-like habitats. It is larger than the Vervet Monkey, with black shoulders, legs and tail. Highly social animals, they form harem troops varying in number. Omnivorous. Diurnal and very shy, they spend most of their time in trees.

Shoulder Height	Active Period	
♂±39cm ♀±35cm		
Mass		
♂±9.3kg ♀±4.9kg		±8cm / ±9.5cm F / H

Habitat	Food

Small Mammals

Although a huge variety of smaller mammals occur in Kruger, only a selection of those a tourist is most likely to see are included here:

The rodents make up the largest diversity of mammals in the world. The largest rodent in Southern Africa is the nocturnal Cape Porcupine, which is widely distributed in the Park. The diurnal Tree Squirrel is the rodent tourists are most likely to see. It occurs virtually everywhere in the Park and may often been seen in the rest camps. The dormice superficially resemble squirrels, but they are much smaller and mainly nocturnal. Their bushy tails distinguish them from other mice and rats. The Greater Canerat is confined to tall riverine vegetation. In spite of its name, the nocturnal Springhare is a rodent, not a true hare.

The nocturnal Scrub Hare is widespread in the Park. It is most likely to be seen on a night drive. The Cape Hare and the Natal Red Rock Rabbit occur in the far northern regions. Peters' Epauletted Fruit Bat is the most likely bat to be recognised of the more than three dozen species that have been recorded in Kruger. The Rock Hyrax occurs mainly in the central regions. It is replaced by the Yellow-spotted Rock Hyrax in the far north.

Other small mammals such as the Ground Pangolin, South African Hedgehog, African Mole-rat, shrews, elephant-shrews and golden moles are not likely to be seen.

Tree Squirrel
Paraxerus cepapi
Boomeekhoring
Common and widespread in the Lowveld. The colour is greyish-brown with yellowish flanks and legs. The tail is long and bushy. Tree Squirrels live in family groups, scent marking and grooming each other to make their presence known. They often mock a predator from a safe distance with bird-like chattering and a flicking tail.

Length	Active
♂±36cm ♀±35cm	Period
Mass	
♂±0.19kg ♀±0.2kg	

Habitat Food

Ulrich Oberprieler

Woodland Dormouse
Graphiurus murinus
Boswaaierstertmuis
These small, greyish rodents have bushy tails and dark brown patches around the eyes. They live in family groups, are extremely territorial and have a very aggressive nature (they will eat an intruder if caught). Nocturnal and tree-living. Omnivorous. May be seen in the rest camps and around other human habitation.

Length	Active
±16cm	Period
Mass	
♂±28g ♀±27g	

Habitat Food

Naas Rautenbach

Small Mammals

Burger Cillié

Cape Porcupine
Hystrix africaeaustralis
Suider-Afrikaanse Ystervark
The largest rodent in Southern Africa. It has characteristic sharp, black-and-white ringed quills that cover most of the body. The shoulder area is covered with long bristle-like hair. Nocturnal and very adaptable; lives in family groups. When threatened it attacks sideways or backwards with its quills facing the enemy.

Length	Active
♂±70cm ♀±72cm	Period
Mass	
♂±15kg ♀±17kg	

Habitat	Food

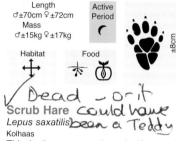
±8cm

[handwritten: Dead – or it Scrub Hare could have been a Teddy]

Scrub Hare
Lepus saxatilis
Kolhaas
This is the common hare in Kruger. It has a white belly with greyish-brown upperparts and large ears. Nocturnal, it emerges at sunset to forage. Usually solitary. Common in savanna and grassland. Often seen on night drives where it continues to run in front of the vehicle. It squeals when in distress and runs fast with swerving movements.

Length	Active
♂±56cm ♀±58cm	Period
Mass	
♂±1.9kg ♀±2.2kg	

Habitat	Food

Ulrich Oberprieler

±3.5cm

Springhare
Pedetes capensis
Springhaas
The Springhare resembles a small kangaroo with its long hindlegs and short forelegs. It has a long, furry tail that ends in a characteristic black tip. Strictly nocturnal. It prefers areas with loose or sandy soil, usually close to rivers. It lives in a burrow that slopes down for a few metres before levelling out. Sometimes seen on night drives.

Length	Active
♂±81cm ♀±80cm	Period
Mass	
♂±3.1kg ♀±2.8kg	

Habitat	Food

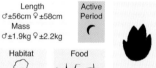

±4cm F
±5cm H

Clem Haagner

Rock Hyrax (Rock Dassie)
Procavia capensis
Klipdassie

Small brown animals with short legs and no tail. They live colonially on rocky areas with sufficient shelter. They are very good climbers and even climb trees for food. Early in the morning a female will be posted as a lookout, while the others bask in the sun or forage. (The Yellow-spotted Rock Hyrax occurs in the Pafuri / Punda Maria area).

Length ♂±53cm ♀±51cm Mass ♂±3.5kg ♀±3.1kg	Active Period	±4cm
Habitat 	Food 	±5.5cm H

Niel Cillié

Peters' Epauletted Fruit Bat
Epomophorus gambianus crypturus
Peters-witkolvrugtevlermuis

A well-known fruit bat that may be encountered under roofs in the rest camps. Their heads are dog-like. Smaller and usually browner than Wahlberg's Epauletted Fruit Bat. Males are larger than females with "epaulettes" of long white hair on the shoulders. The males' monotonous "ping" sounds at night give away their presence.

Length ±15cm Mass ♂±104g ♀±76g	Active Period	NO SPOOR
Habitat	Food	

Burger Cillié

Acacia Rat
Thallomys paedulcus
Boommuis

These nocturnal tree-dwellers are greyish-brown with conspicuous white underparts. The tail is about the same length as the body and head, and is used for balancing when climbing in a tree. They occur in open acacia savanna or woodland. During the day a family group rests in their large conspicuous grass nest in a tree.

Length ±27cm Mass ♂±76g ♀±68g	Active Period	±0.9cm
Habitat	Food	

Naas Rautenbach

Small Mammals

Niel Cillié

Greater Canerat
Thryonomys swinderianus
Grootrietrot
Although being rodents, canerats are not rats at all. They resemble dassies, have short tails, rounded noses and spiny fur. Mainly nocturnal. Usually found near vleis and rivers, they are good swimmers. They feed on stems and sprouts of reeds and grass. Canerats live in groups consisting of a male, two or more females and their offspring.

Length	Active
♂±72cm ♀±67cm	Period
Mass	
♂±4.5kg ♀±3.6kg	

Habitat   Food

±8cm

Naas Rautenbach

Bushveld Gerbil
Tatera leucogaster
Bosveldnagmuis
The nocturnal Bushveld Gerbil has big eyes and a silky reddish-brown fur. It is common and widely distributed in the Lowveld. It digs burrows, the entrance of which is usually characterised by a fresh heap of soil from the previous night's activity. Although these burrows may be regarded as communal, this rodent is solitary and not social.

Length	Active
±28cm	Period
Mass	
♂±71g ♀±68g	

Habitat   Food

±0.8cm

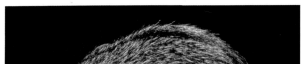

Naas Rautenbach

Single-striped Grass Mouse
Lemniscomys rosalia
Eenstreepmuis
A medium-sized mouse. It is orange-brown with a characteristic single dark brown stripe down its back. This terrestrial mouse lives in burrows which it may excavate itself. It prefers woodland and plains with a good cover of grass. Diurnal. This nervous animal is reluctant to bite and occasionally plays dead when handled.

Length	Active
±27cm	Period
Mass	
±58g	

Habitat   Food

±1cm

BIRDS

Birds are warm-blooded animals covered with feathers. Most species have the ability to fly. Birdwatching is a fascinating hobby enjoyed by many visitors to the Park. In this book birds are divided into the following groups for easy reference

Swimming and Diving Waterbirds

Grebes, moorhen, geese, ducks, cormorants and darters

Larger Birds with Long Legs

Ostrich, Hamerkop, herons, egrets, storks, ibises, spoonbills, bustards and korhaans

Smaller Birds with Long Legs

Crakes, jacanas, plovers, lapwings, stilts, sandpiper, thick-knees (dikkop) and coursers

Gamebirds (Fowl-like Birds)

Guineafowl, sandgrouse, spurfowl and francolin

Raptors (Birds of Prey)

Owls, eagles, snake-eagles, kites, fish-eagles, Secretarybird, buzzards, goshawks and vultures

Fruiteaters

Mousebirds, turacos (louries), green-pigeons, parrots, barbets and tinkerbirds

BIRDS

Birds with Long, Straight Bills

Kingfishers and woodpeckers

Birds with Long, Decurved Bills

Hornbills, hoopoes, wood-hoopoes, bee-eaters and sunbirds

Aerial insectivores

Nightjars, swallows and swifts

Insectivores with Stout Bills

Crows, coucals, rollers, tchagras and shrikes

Insectivores with Medium-sized Bills

Cuckoos, drongos, flycatchers, tits, orioles, babblers, thrushes, robin-chats, scrub-robins, cliff-chats, batis, bulbuls, greenbuls, pipits, longclaws, larks, wagtails, oxpeckers and starlings

Small Insectivores with Tiny Bills

White-eyes, crombecs, camaropteras, prinias, apalis, tit-babblers and cisticolas

Seedeaters

Sparrows, weavers, petronias, waxbills, firefinches, bishops, queleas, pytilias, mannikins, canaries, buntings, whydahs, widowbirds and doves

Swimming and Diving Waterbirds

These waterbirds are relatively large and fairly easy to identify. Although one may see them in flight or resting on the water's edge, they are usually observed swimming on the water, while some species even dive in pursuit of prey. For this reason the legs are short and the toes are webbed, except in the grebes and moorhen which have flat, lobed toes.

A variety of Southern African ducks and geese may be seen in the Lowveld after the summer rains have filled the dams, pans and rivers. As their numbers thus fluctuate greatly between seasons and also from year to year, only three of the more conspicuous and permanent species are discussed in this guide.

The cormorants and darters are mostly dark in colour. They swim very low in the water due to the fact that their plumage is not waterproof and thus lacks buoyancy. They dive frequently for their food. After swimming they have to dry their feathers by sunning themselves with outstreched wings.

The grebes and moorhen may be mistaken for ducks, but are characterised by their pointed bills. Grebes dive to catch small prey, while the moorhen are mainly vegetarian.

Little Grebe (Dabchick)
Tachybaptus ruficollis **8**
Kleindobbertjie

Pigeon-sized: smaller than any duck. The only grebe found in the Park. In breeding birds the chestnut sides of the neck and the pale spot on the base of the bill are diagnostic. Non-breeding and immature birds are smoky-grey. Commonly found on quiet stretches of water. Dives frequently and remains submerged for up to 50 seconds.

Food	Nest	Active Period
	1-5	

Habitat	Sociability	Migration

Common Moorhen
Gallinula chloropus **226**
Grootwaterhoender

Larger than a pigeon. This moorhen is slaty black all over, except for white undertail feathers and white streaks on the flanks. The red frontal shield and bill ending in a yellow tip are diagnostic. Young birds are greyish. Inhabits reedbeds and sedges, but frequently swims in open water or wades in the shallows. Flicks its tail when alarmed.

Food	Nest	Active Period
	2-7	

Habitat	Sociability	Migration

Egyptian Goose
Alopochen aegyptiaca 102
Kolgans
Well known: a large brown goose; slightly larger than a guineafowl. The dark brown patches around the eyes and on the centre of the chest are characteristic. The large white wing panels are conspicuous in flight. Immature birds are duller, the eye-patches are smaller and the chest-patch usually absent. Females honk noisily; males hiss.

Food	Nest	Active Period
	5-11	

Habitat	Sociability	Migration

Spur-winged Goose
Plectropterus gambensis 116
Wildemakou
The largest goose in Southern Africa; much larger than a guineafowl. Mainly black with variable amount of white on the underparts and head. The bill and legs are pinkish red. Males are larger than females and have a growth on the forehead. Occur in the Park mainly after the summer rains when they prefer areas of shallow water. Usually occur in flocks.

Food	Nest	Active Period
	6-12	

Habitat	Sociability	Migration

Comb Duck (Knob-billed Duck)
Sarkidiornis melanotos 115
Knobbeleend
A large black-and-white duck; about the size of a guineafowl. The speckled head contrasts with the blue-black upperparts and the white underparts. Males are larger than females with a black knob on the bill that enlarges during the breeding season. Males often mate with more than one female. Perches in trees or on the ground.

Food	Nest	Active Period
	6-20	

Habitat	Sociability	Migration

White-breasted Cormorant
Phalacrocorax lucidus 55
Witborsduiker

Larger than a guineafowl. Adult birds are mostly black with a white throat and chest. May show white thigh-patches while breeding. Differs from the similar Reed Cormorant by its larger size and heavier bill. The immature bird's underparts are completely white. Swims with its body partially submerged and dives for fish. Often flies low over the water.

Food	Nest	Active Period
	1-4	

Habitat	Sociability	Migration

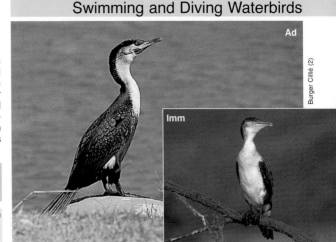

Ad

Imm

Burger Cillié (2)

Reed Cormorant
Phalacrocorax africanus 58
Rietduiker

Smaller than a guineafowl. Differs from the White-breasted Cormorant by its much smaller size, the slender bill and the long tail. The underparts appear very dark in breeding adults, mottled in non-breeding adults and off-white in immature birds. After swimming, it often sits in the sun with wings outspread to dry. Dives frequently.

Food	Nest	Active Period
	2-6	

Habitat	Sociability	Migration

Ad

Imm

Ulrich Oberprieler

Niel Cillié

African Darter
Anhinga rufa 60
Afrikaanse Slanghalsvoël

Larger than a guineafowl. The long neck and tail, pointed bill and slender body distinguish it from the cormorants. Breeding adults have white streaks on the wings and the foreneck is chestnut. Non-breeding adults are browner, while immature birds have creamy underparts. Swims partially submerged with only the head and neck showing.

Food	Nest	Active Period
	2-7	

Habitat	Sociability	Migration

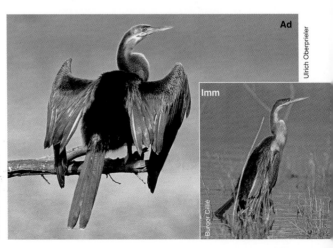

Ad

Imm

Ulrich Oberprieler

Burger Cillié

Larger Birds with Long Legs

These birds are larger than guineafowl and are characterised by their long legs. The wading birds are associated with water or other moist habitats where their long legs are of great benefit. These are the Hamerkop, herons, egrets, storks, ibises en spoonbills.

The Hamerkop, an uniquely African bird, is easily identified. The herons and closely related egrets have long, sharply pointed bills. Most develop long ornate plumes on the head and chest during the breeding season. Although all species have long necks, some tend to tuck their heads between their shoulders and thus appear to be short-necked. All species hold their necks folded in flight and are thus readily distinguished from similar birds.

The storks are very large birds with long, heavy bills and boldly coloured plumages. They are nearly voiceless, but communicate by clapping their bills. Ibises are characterised by their long decurved bills used to probe in mud and soil, while the African Spoonbill's uniquely shaped bill makes it unmistakable.

Other birds in this group are adapted to an existence in drier terrestrial habitats. The bustards and korhaans have brown, well-camouflaged backs, but their underparts are usually boldly coloured. They have only three toes per foot.

Common Ostrich
Struthio camelus 1
Volstruis

Well known and unmistakable. Males are black with white wings and tails whereas females and immature birds are brownish grey. They are able to sprint up to 60 km/h. Males often mate with more than one female and may perform elaborate displays during courtship. The booming call sounds like the distant roar of a lion.

Food	Nest	Active Period
	4-26	

Habitat	Sociability	Migration

Hamerkop
Scopus umbretta 81
Hamerkop

Guineafowl-sized. The hammer-shaped head and the strong bill of this brown bird are diagnostic. Forages in or around shallow water; sometimes stirring the mud with its feet to disturb small prey. The nest is an enormous structure of sticks and grasses, built in a tree or on a rock. This common resident always keeps close to rivers and dams.

Food	Nest	Active Period
	UNIQUE	
	1-5	

Habitat	Sociability	Migration

Grey Heron
Ardea cinerea 62
Bloureier

A large heron. The black band above the eyes and the white crown distinguish it from the uncommon Black-headed Heron, which has a black cap extending to below the eyes. The bill and legs are yellowish. In flight the underwings are uniform grey. Immatures are paler. Wades in shallow water and stands for long periods in wait for prey.

Ad

Imm

Niel Cillié

Ulrich Oberprieler

Food	Nest	Active Period
	2-3	
Habitat	Sociability	Migration

Goliath Heron
Ardea goliath 64
Reusereier

The Park's largest heron has a heavy bill. The back and wings are grey, and the neck, crown and underparts are chestnut. The bill, legs and feet are dark grey. Immatures are browner with buff underparts. Stands motionless for long periods in deeper water, waiting for prey. In flight, the long legs tend to hang down slightly.

Burger Cillié

Food	Nest	Active Period
	2-7	
Habitat	Sociability	Migration

Green-backed Heron
Butorides striata 74
Groenrugreier

Smaller than a guineafowl. The black crown, yellow legs, shiny greenish-grey back and white-edged feathers on the wings are diagnostic. The immature bird is brown with white streaks on the neck and spots on the wings. Prefers areas with dense vegetation close to water. Often fishes from branches overhanging the water. Shy, but fairly common.

Ad

Imm

Burger Cillié

Lizeth Cillié

Food	Nest	Active Period
	2-7	
Habitat	Sociability	Migration

NBr

Br

Burger Cillié (2)

Great Egret (Great White Egret)
Egretta alba 66
Grootwitreier
The largest of the white egrets; nearly the size of a Grey Heron. It has a very long neck and long black legs and toes. The bill is yellow, but turns black during the beginning of the breeding season. A dark line extends from the gape to at least 1cm behind the eye. Stands motionless in water for long periods. Common and widespread.

Food	Nest	Active Period
	2-5	☼

Habitat	Sociability	Migration

NBr

Br

Niel Cillié

Burger Cillié

Cattle Egret
Bubulcus ibis 71
Veereier (Bosluisvoël)
Well known; the smallest of the white egrets. Adult birds have yellow bills and legs. During breeding they have orange-pinkish plumes on the head, back and chest. Immatures have black bills, legs and feet. Forage in flocks and are usually seen with larger herbivores such as African Buffalo. They fly in a V-formation to and from roosting sites along rivers.

Food	Nest	Active Period
	1-7	☼

Habitat	Sociability	Migration

Burger Cillié

Squacco Heron
(Common Squacco Heron)
Ardeola ralloides 72
Ralreier
About the size of a Cattle Egret, but more robust. This buffy-brown heron has dark stripes on the neck, a streaky drooping crest and a yellowish bill that turns blue with a black tip when breeding. The brilliant white wings are conspicuous in flight. A shy bird that is easily overlooked it forages in shallow, quiet water.

Food	Nest	Active Period
	2-7	☼

Habitat	Sociability	Migration

White Stork
Ciconia ciconia **83**
Witooievaar

A very large bird. The White Stork has a white body and tail, and black flight feathers. The red legs and shorter red bill distinguish it from the Yellow-billed Stork. They defecate on their legs to cool down and therefore the legs may appear white or grey. Groups spiral high in the air in search of food. Roost communally in trees.

Food	Nest	Active Period
	**EUROPE**	☀

Habitat	Sociability	Migration
		◯

Yellow-billed Stork
Mycteria ibis **90**
Nimmersat

A very large bird. The Yellow-billed Stork has a bare red face and a long yellow bill that is slightly decurved at the tip. It has a black tail and flight feathers. The white feathers on the wings are slightly pinkish when breeding. The immature bird is greyish with an orange face. Found in larger stretches of water where it forages for fish and other prey,

Ad

Imm

Food	Nest	Active Period
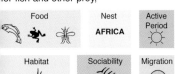	**AFRICA**	☀

Habitat	Sociability	Migration
		◯

Woolly-necked Stork
Ciconia episcopus **86**
Wolnekooievaar

A very large bird. The glossy black back and wings, and the white woolly neck are characteristic. The face is mostly black. In flight, the white undertail coverts project beyond the black tail. Immature birds are duller. Forages at the water's edge by walking slowly or standing motionless for long periods. Prefers swampy wooded regions.

Food	Nest	Active Period
	2-4	☀

Habitat	Sociability	Migration
		◯

41

Larger Birds with Long Legs

African Openbill
(African Open-billed Stork)
Anastomus lamelligerus 87
Oopbekooievaar

A very large bird. It has a characteristic large bill with a distinct gap between the upper and lower jaws. The plumage is very dark and the legs are black. The immature is duller with a straight bill without a gap. Solitary; forages in quiet water for snails and mussels. Roosts in trees.

Food	Nest	Active Period
	3-9	

Habitat	Sociability	Migration

Saddle-billed Stork
Ephippiorhynchus senegalensis 88
Saalbekooievaar

A very large, black-and-white stork. The huge black-and-red bill with its yellow saddle at the base is characteristic. Males are characterised by their dark eyes and the small yellow wattles or the chin. The female has yellow eyes. The immature is grey-brown with a dark brown bill. Roosts in trees, but forages in shallow water.

Food	Nest	Active Period
	1-8	

Habitat	Sociability	Migration

Marabou Stork
Leptoptilus cruminiferus 89
Maraboe

A very large stork with dark grey upperparts and white underparts. The bare pinkish neck and head are characteristic. It has a large bill and long white legs. Mainly a scavenger, it is often seen in the company of vultures. Common in the vicinity of rubbish dumps near rest camps. Defecates on its legs to cool down.

Food	Nest	Active Period
	AFRICA	

Habitat	Sociability	Migration

Glossy Ibis
Plegadis falcinellus 93
Glansibis

Guineafowl-sized. A slender, brick-brown ibis with a green sheen on the back and wings. Superficially similar to the Hadeda Ibis, it has a longer, thinner neck and a more slender, decurved bill. In non-breeding birds the head and neck are spotted white. Prefers shallow flooded areas, such as marshes and floodplains. Usually in flocks.

Food	Nest	Active Period
	2-4	☀

Habitat	Sociability	Migration
		●

Ad

Imm

Burger Cillié (2)

Hadeda Ibis
Bostrychia hagedash 94
Hadeda

Guineafowl-sized. A greyish-brown, compact ibis with an iridescent green sheen on the wings. The long dark bill has a red ridge on top. A white stripe runs from the bill base to behind the eye. Immatures lack the red bill and glossy wings. Utters the characteristic loud "ha-ha-hadeda" call when disturbed. Widespread in the Park, usually near water.

Food	Nest	Active Period
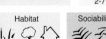	2-7	☀

Habitat	Sociability	Migration
		●

Ulrich Oberprieler

African Spoonbill
Platalea alba 95
Afrikaanse Lepelaar

This large white bird has a characteristic spoon-shaped bill. The long legs and bare face are red. The immature has a dull yellowish bill and greyish legs. Forages by wading slowly in shallow water, moving its bill from side to side. Feeds mostly on small fish and aquatic invertebrates. Rather shy. Roosts in colonies in trees or reedbeds.

Food	Nest	Active Period
	2-6	☀

Habitat	Sociability	Migration
		●

Burger Cillié

43

Larger Birds with Long Legs

Burger Cillié

Kori Bustard
Ardeotis kori 230
Gompou
Large and unmistakable. This bustard has a crested head with a greyish barred neck. The back and wings are pale brown and the belly is white. The female is smaller than the male, which has an elaborate courtship display. It prefers open grassy areas where it walks slowly with its bill held slightly upwards. Breeds on the ground.

Food	Nest	Active Period
🦟 🌾	NONE 1-2	☀

Habitat	Sociability	Migration

Burger Cillié
Niel Cillié

Red-crested Korhaan
Lophotis ruficrista 237
Boskorhaan
Guineafowl-sized. The white "V"-marks on the back and wings are diagnostic. The female has a brown head and the male a blue-grey head and neck. His belly is black with two white patches on the chest. The male's reddish crest is only visible during courtship when he flies vertically upwards and tumbles straight down. Breeds on the ground.

Food	Nest	Active Period
🦟 🌾 🍎	NONE 1-2	☀

Habitat	Sociability	Migration

Ulrich Oberprieler (2)

Black-bellied Bustard
(Black-bellied Korhaan)
Lissotis melanogaster 238
Langbeenkorhaan
It has long legs and a long thin neck, and appears larger than the Red-crested Korhaan. It has characteristically shaped black markings on the back. The male has a black belly with black line extending up onto the throat; the female's belly is white. In display the male flies high into the air and glides down.

Food	Nest	Active Period
🦟 🍃	NONE 1-5	☀

Habitat	Sociability	Migration

nlike the previous group, these birds are smaller than guineafowl, but are also characterised by eir long legs. A number of them are usually referred to as waders as they prefer shallow water r other moist environments.

he crakes and jacanas have robust bodies and relatively shorter legs. Their toes, however, are ng, helping them to walk over aquatic vegetation.

he plovers are smallish birds usually found close to water. Their well-camouflaged backs cause em to be overlooked easily. Their larger relatives, the lapwings, are boldly coloured and thus ften seen. Some species are associated with water, while others prefer short grassy, overgrazed r recently burnt patches.

he sandpipers and relatives are never common in the Park, but may be seen in spring and ummer while visiting from the northern hemisphere. They are distinguished from plovers and apwings by their longer bills. Their non-descript plumages make their identification difficult.

he thick-knees are mainly nocturnal. Although two species occur in Kruger, the Water Thick-nee is most often seen on night drives, as is the Bronze-winged Courser. Temminck's Courser is omadic, but may be observed in open, overgrazed areas.

3lack Crake
Amaurornis flavirostris **213**
wartriethaan

\ dove-sized black bird with red legs nd eyes, and a bright yellow-green bill. he immature bird is olive-brown with dark bill. Not as secretive as other rakes and thus often seen in the open, specially after rains. Flicks its tail and valks with jerking movements. Flies low ver water. Sometimes swims. Fairly oisy: a characteristic "k-k-k-krrung".

Food	Nest	Active Period
	2-6	

Habitat	Sociability	Migration
		⬤

Burger Cillié

African Jacana
Actophilornis africanus **240**
3rootlangtoon

Ad

The very long toes enable these pigeon-sized birds to walk over floating vegeta-ion. The body is a rich chestnut with a vhite neck and a black nape. The bill nd frontal shield are blue. The immature ird is paler and has a characteristic eye-stripe. It is much larger than the similar _esser Jacana. The male incubates the eggs and raises the chicks.

Food	Nest	Active Period
	2-5	

Habitat	Sociability	Migration

Niel Cillié

Imm

Burger Cillié

Niel Cillié

Kittlitz's Plover
Charadrius pecuarius 248
Geelborsstrandkiewiet
Shrike-sized. The creamy-brown breas and the black line that runs through th eyes to the nape are distinctive whe breeding. It has longer legs than othe small plovers. The immature bird lack the black forecrown and its underpart are whiter. Prefers extensive shores water bodies. Runs and flies fast. Easil overlooked unless it is moving.

Food	Nest	Active Period
	1-3	

Habitat	Sociability	Migratio

Burger Cillié

Three-banded Plover
Charadrius tricollaris 249
Driebandstrandkiewiet
Shrike-sized. This plover is very commo in the Park. The two black bands o the chest, separated by a white ban are diagnostic. It has a red bill with black tip and red rings around the eye Commonly found on the shoreline most water bodies. Easily overlooke when standing still. Runs fast with quic jerky movements.

Food	Nest	Active Period
	1-2	

Habitat	Sociability	Migratio

Ulrich Oberprieler

Crowned Lapwing
(Crowned Plover)
Vanellus coronatus 255
Kroonkiewiet
An unmistakable dove-sized bird with white "halo" surrounding the black crowr The legs and base of the bill are red. The immature bird is browner. Very commo in areas of short grass. When thei young or eggs are threatened, thes birds attack intruders by dive-bombing them while uttering noisy screams.

Food	Nest	Active Period
	1-4	

Habitat	Sociability	Migratior

enegal Lapwing
Lesser Black-winged Plover)
anellus lugubris 256
einswartvlerkkiewiet

ove-sized. It has a narrow black breast-
and that separates the greyish chest
om the white belly. The small white
atch on the forehead and pale eyes
e diagnostic. Occurs in small flocks
id regularly mixes with other lapwing
ecies. Usually seen in recently burnt
overgrazed areas.

Food	Nest	Active Period
	1-4	
Habitat	Sociability	Migration

Burger Cillié

lacksmith Lapwing
Blacksmith Plover)
anellus armatus 258
ntkiewiet

he black-and-white body makes this
ve-sized bird easy to identify. The
mature bird is browner and has less
hite on the forehead. Occurs through-
ut the Park, usually close to water. The
ame refers to the alarm call, sounding
e a blacksmith's hammer striking an
nvil.

Food	Nest	Active Period
	2-6	
Habitat	Sociability	Migration

Niel Cillié

White-crowned Lapwing
White-crowned Plover)
anellus albiceps 259
itkopkiewiet

ove-sized. It has long yellow wattles
ith a white band across the crown. The
hite (not brown) chest distinguishes it
om the African Wattled Plover. A white
ripe runs between the brown back and
ack wing. In flight the wings are white.
shy and wary bird. It occurs on the
andbanks of the larger rivers.

Food	Nest	Active Period
	2-4	
Habitat	Sociability	Migration

Ulrich Oberprieler

47

Burger Cillié

Black-winged Stilt
Himantopus himantopus 295
Rooipootelsie
This black-and-white wader has characteristic thin pointed black bill. Th extremely long, red legs project we beyond the tail in flight. The immatu bird is grey on the head and nape. prefers shallow water where it forage by picking food from the surface. Ofte goes belly-deep into the water. Occur widely in the Park.

Food	Nest	Active Period
	4	

Habitat	Sociability	Migratic

Ulrich Oberprieler

Common Sandpiper
Actitis hypoleucos 264
Gewone Ruiter
A small wader, smaller than a dove. differs from the Wood Sandpiper in that shows an obvious white shoulder-patc in front of the closed wings, has short legs and a plain, dark brown back. frequently bobs its body and tail u and down. Solitary on the water's edg where it may easily be overlooked. flies low over water with flickering wir beats.

Food	Nest	Active Period
	EURASIA	

Habitat	Sociability	Migrati

Ulrich Oberprieler

Wood Sandpiper
Tringa glareola 266
Bosruiter
A smallish wader, smaller than a dov The spotted upperparts, white eyebro and yellow-green legs distinguish it fro the Common Sandpiper. The white rum and tail, with dark bars, are visible flight. When flushed, this sandpiper flie a short distance before settling agai bobbing its body up and down. Easi overlooked when standing still.

Food	Nest	Active Period
	EURASIA	

Habitat	Sociability	Migratic

Marsh Sandpiper
Tringa stagnatilis 269

Moerasruiter

Easily confused with the Common Greenshank, but it is smaller and has a straight, much thinner bill. The face and underparts are white, the upperparts greyish. Wades in slightly deeper water and may feed with its head submerged. Moves quickly, but is not as wary as the Common Greenshank. Usually solitary, but mixes with other waders.

Food	Nest	Active Period
	EURASIA	

Habitat	Sociability	Migration

Burger Cillié

Common Greenshank
Tringa nebularia 270

Groenpootruiter

Larger than a dove. It is slightly darker and much larger than the similar Marsh Sandpiper. The grey bill is heavier and slightly upcurved. The underparts and face are white, the upperparts greyish. The dark line extending from the bill to the eyes is diagnostic. Unlike the Marsh Sandpiper, this is a shy and wary bird. Often enters deeper water.

Food	Nest	Active Period
	EURASIA	

Habitat	Sociability	Migration

Burger Cillié

Ruff (female = Reeve)
Philomachus pugnax 284

Kemphaan

About dove-sized. Both sexes have a diagnostic scaled pattern on the upperparts and wings. The colour of the legs varies between individuals from greenish to orange-brown. The female, known as Reeve, is much smaller than the male. Forages by sweeping the bill from side to side or stabbing quickly at its prey. Usually seen in flocks.

Food	Nest	Active Period
	EURASIA	

Habitat	Sociability	Migration

Niel Cillié

49

Water Thick-knee
(Water Dikkop)
Burhinus vermiculatus 298
Waterdikkop

Larger than a dove. It differs from the Spotted Thick-knee in that the upperparts are streaked and the grey wing-bar that is conspicuously edged with black. The legs and eyes are yellow-green. A nocturnal bird, but is also seen during the day. Prefers to run when disturbed, but may also fly.

Food	Nest	Active Period
	1-2	

Habitat	Sociability	Migration

Temminck's Courser
Cursorius temminckii 300
Trekdrawwertjie

It is smaller than the other coursers (smaller than a dove). The entire crown, upper belly and upperparts are rufous. A dark brown patch on the belly extends to between the legs. Usually found in recently burnt veld or overgrazed areas. When alarmed it moves the body up and down by flexing its legs. Nomadic. Breeds on the ground.

Food	Nest	Active Period
	NONE 1-2	

Habitat	Sociability	Migration

Bronze-winged Courser
Rhinoptilus chalcopterus 303
Bronsvlerkdrawwertjie

About dove-sized. The dark brown band across the chest, bold white-and-brown facial pattern and red legs are characteristic. In flight the white rump and white wing bar are conspicuous. Mainly nocturnal, it is easily overlooked during the day as it roosts in the shade of a tree. When disturbed it may crouch. Breeds on the ground.

Food	Nest	Active Period
	NONE 2-3	

Habitat	Sociability	Migration

The fowl-like gamebirds are well known as they remind us of domestic chicken. They are mostly ground-living birds that fly reluctantly. The bown colour camouflages them well (except the guineafowl).

Both Southern African guineafowl occur in the Park. The Helmeted Guineafowl is widespread throughout, while the Crested Guineafowl may be seen mainly in the Pafuri area. Both guineafowl are characterised by their dark plumages, which are spotted and streaked with paler colours.

The most important way to identify the various francolin and spurfowl is by looking at the pattern on their underparts. The larger spurfowl are characterised by their screeching, raucous calls. When approached they usually run away before taking to the air. The smaller francolin on the other hand, have clearer whistling calls. They rely on their camouflaging colours by squatting when disturbed.

The pigeon-like sandgrouse are essentially birds of arid regions. For this reason only one species, the Double-banded Sandgrouse, is found in the Park. They are not easily seen except at sunset when large numbers congregate at waterholes to drink.

Helmeted Guineafowl
Numida meleagris 203
Gewone Tarentaal

Well known. Differs from the Crested Guineafowl in the naked blue head, red crown and pale brown, horny casque. The casque differs in size between individuals, being most well developed in adult males. They forage in open areas by scratching for food with their feet. Although mainly terrestrial, they like to roost in huge trees.

Food	Nest	Active Period
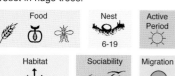	6-19	

Habitat	Sociability	Migration

Ulrich Oberprieler

Crested Guineafowl
Guttera edouardi 204
Kuifkoptarentaal

The curly black feathers on the crown and the pale band on the wing distinguish it from the Helmeted Guineafowl. It has a black neck and body with white spots, and greyish face with conspicuous red eyes. Not as common as the Helmeted Guineafowl. Prefers very dense wooded vegetation. Most easily seen in the Pafuri area.

Food	Nest	Active Period
	4-6	

Habitat	Sociability	Migration

Niel Cillié

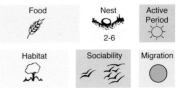

Niel Cillié (2)

Double-banded Sandgrouse
Pterocles bicinctus **347**
Dubbelbandsandpatrys

Pigeon-sized. The male has black and white bands on the forehead and an orange-yellow bill. A set of black and white bands separate the green-brown chest from the barred belly. The female is paler with almost the entire body finely barred. More common in the northern parts of the Park. Large numbers congregate at waterholes at sunset.

Food	Nest	Active Period
	2-6	

Habitat	Sociability	Migration

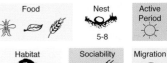

Niel Cillié

Natal Spurfowl
(Natal Francolin)
Pternistis natalensis **196**
Natalse Fisant

It has a white-scaled belly and flanks. Its orange-red bill and legs are diagnostic. The immature bird is duller than the adult and brownish below. It prefers thickets, often close to water, and is common in the Park. When flushed, it runs into dense cover or flies a short distance, and may settle in a tree.

Food	Nest	Active Period
	5-8	

Habitat	Sociability	Migration

Niel Cillié

Swainson's Spurfowl
(Swainson's Francolin)
Pternistis swainsonii **199**
Bosveldfisant

The red throat and bare red eye-patch, dark bill and dark legs distinguish it from other spurfowl. The whole body is brownish and covered with black stripes. A wary bird, it will seek cover in dense vegetation when disturbed. Very common in the Park. The raucous, crowing call is heard at dawn and dusk.

Food	Nest	Active Period
	4-12	

Habitat	Sociability	Migration

Coqui Francolin
Peliperdix coqui 188

Swempie

A small francolin. The male is easily distinguished from other francolin: the head and neck are golden brown with a darker crown. The female has white eyebrows and a white throat outlined in black. The belly of both sexes is heavily marked with black and white bars. A secretive bird that usually crouches when disturbed. Calls "co-qui co-qui".

Food	Nest	Active Period
	3-8	

Habitat	Sociability	Migration

♂

♀

Christo Joubert

Ulrich Oberprieler

Crested Francolin
Dendroperdix sephaena 189

Bospatrys

The triangular dark markings on the chest, white eyebrows and reddish legs are diagnostic. The dark crest is only raised when alarmed. The only francolin in the Park that runs with its tail cocked like a bantam. Very vocal at dusk and dawn when uttering the distinctive "beer-and-cognac" call. Often seen feeding by the roadside.

Food	Nest	Active Period
	4-9	

Habitat	Sociability	Migration

Burger Cillié

Shelley's Francolin
Scleroptila shelleyi 191

Laeveldpatrys

This smallish francolin has a white throat edged with a thin black stripe. The heavy bill, chestnut-streaked flanks and chest, and the black and white bars on the belly are diagnostic. Usually calls early in the morning and late afternoon: "I'll-drink-your-beer, I'll-drink-your-beer". Shy and secretive. Prefers thickets around koppies.

Food	Nest	Active Period
	3-8	

Habitat	Sociability	Migration

Burger Cillié

53

Raptors (Birds of Prey)

The raptors are characterised by their hooked bills and sharp claws. Most of them are active predators, but vultures are specialised scavengers. Owls are active at night while the other raptors hunt during the day.

The Park is home to a variety of owls, the most conspicuous of which are described in this guide. Owls are more often heard than seen: it thus makes sense to familiarise oneself with their characteristic calls.

A number of large, eagle-like raptors occur in the Park. The true eagles are characterised by their fully feathered legs, while both snake-eagles and fish-eagles have unfeathered lower legs. Snake-eagles are distinguished by their relatively large heads and large eyes.

Vultures are huge scavenging birds with bare heads. Unlike other large soaring raptors with long broad wings, vultures have relatively short tails. They congregate in large numbers at carcasses.

The medium-sized and smaller raptors are represented by a large number of species. As their identification is not easy and often requires detailed knowledge, only the more recognisable species are described in this guide.

Burger Cillié

Verreaux's Eagle-Owl
(Giant Eagle-Owl)
Bubo lacteus **402**
Reuse-ooruil

Easily distinguished from other large owls by its grey colour (Pel's Fishing-Owl is tawny) and its dark eyes with pink eyelids. Immature birds are slightly brownish. It rarely hunts during the day, but roosts in a large shady tree. The call is a deep grunt. Breeds on the nest of other birds.

Food	Nest	Active Period
	NONE	
	1-2	

Habitat	Sociability	Migration

Niel Cillié

Spotted Eagle-Owl
Bubo africanus **401**
Gevlekte Ooruil

This large greyish-brown owl is characterised by the yellow eyes, barred underparts and, like all eagle-owls, the conspicuous ear-tufts. Common and widespread. Its duet call is often heard in rest camps: the male's "hu-hooo" is answered by the female's "hoo" call. During the day it roosts in trees and amongst rocks. Breeds in various suitable places.

Food	Nest	Active Period
	NONE	
	2-4	

Habitat	Sociability	Migration

African Scops-Owl
Otus senegalensis 396
Skopsuil
A very small, well-camouflaged owl with ear-tufts and yellow eyes. The colour pattern resembles tree bark, which makes it difficult to spot. The smaller size and grey face distinguishes it from the Southern White-faced Scops-Owl. It is a common resident in the Park where its insect-like "prrrrup" call is often heard at night.

Food	Nest	Active Period
	 2-3	

Habitat	Sociability	Migration

Arthur Hall

Ulrich Oberprieler

Camouflaged

Southern White-faced Scops-Owl (White-faced Owl)
Ptilopsis granti 397
Witwanguil
This smallish owl differs from the African Scops-Owl in that it has orange eyes and a white facial disk edged with black. When disturbed, it elongates its body and closes its eyes to slits to camouflage itself. The call is a fast and dove-like hooting "do-do-do-do-hohoo". Breeds mostly on the nests of other birds.

Food	Nest	Active Period
	NONE 2-4	

Habitat	Sociability	Migration

Ulrich Oberprieler (2)

Camouflaged

Pearl-spotted Owlet
Glaucidium perlatum 398
Witkoluil
A very small round-headed owl with a whitish face and yellow eyes. The upperparts are brown with white spots. At the back of the head are two dark spots edged with white. The white underparts are streaked brown. It stares at intruders and flicks its tail when alarmed. The characteristic whistling call may be heard even during the day.

Food	Nest	Active Period
	 2-4	

Habitat	Sociability	Migration

Burger Cillié

Raptors (Birds of Prey)

Lizeth Cillié

Ulrich Oberprieler

Tawny Eagle
Aquila rapax 132
Roofarend

eating prey

Difficult to distinguish from other large brown eagles; as large as a fish-eagle. The colour is usually rufous or tawny brown, but different colour variations occur, from dark brown to very pale. The gape extends to just below the eye, not to behind the eye as in the Steppe Eagle. It has a wide range of feeding habits and will hunt from a perch or in flight.

Food	Nest	Active Period
	1-3	

Habitat	Sociability	Migration

Ad

Niel Cillié (2)

Pale form

Wahlberg's Eagle
Aquila wahlbergi 135
Wahlberg-arend

The most common small brown eagle in the Park during summer; smaller than a fish-eagle. The slender body and long square tail may help to identify this bird. There are different colour forms, from dark to pale brown. The eyes are always dark brown. The head is often slightly crested. Prefers to perch in leafy trees and is easily overlooked.

Food	Nest	Active Period
	1	

Habitat	Sociability	Migration

Burger Cillié

Brown Snake-Eagle
Circaetus cinereus 142
Bruinslangarend

Unlike true eagles, snake-eagles have bare creamy-white legs and large heads with large yellow eyes. Adult Brown Snake-Eagles are dark brown, while immatures are slightly mottled. This is one of the more common larger raptors in the Park. It usually hunts from a perch, dropping onto the prey. Its diet consists mainly of snakes.

Food	Nest	Active Period
	1	

Habitat	Sociability	Migration

Black-chested Snake-Eagle
Circaetus pectoralis 143
Swartborsslangarend
Easily confused with the much larger Martial Eagle, but the lower legs are unfeathered and the belly is pure white. The underwing appears white in flight. Immatures may be confused with Brown Snake-Eagles, but are more rufous or tawny-brown. Hunts from a perch or during hovering flight. Feeds mostly on snakes.

Food	Nest	Active Period
	1	

Habitat	Sociability	Migration

Martial Eagle
Polemaetus bellicosus 140
Breëkoparend
A very large eagle with dark brown upperparts, head and neck. The belly is white with dark brown spots and the legs are white. The underwings appear dark in flight. The immature bird is much paler with completely white underparts. Spends most of the day soaring high and is therefore less often seen on a perch. Roosts in trees at night.

Food	Nest	Active Period
	1	

Habitat	Sociability	Migration

Bateleur
Terathopius ecaudatus 146
Berghaan
A large, unmistakable raptor. When perched, the female has a pale band on the flight feathers, the male's are dark. The very short tail is apparent in flight. The male then shows a broad and the female a narrow black trailing edge to the wing. The immature is brown, but has the same body shape as the adults. Often seen soaring in the air.

Food	Nest	Active Period
	1	

Habitat	Sociability	Migration

Raptors (Birds of Prey)

Niel Cillié (2)

Ad

Imm

Yellow-billed Kite
Milvus migrans parasitus 126b
Geelbekwou
This medium-sized raptor has a brown plumage and a deeply forked tail. Adults have yellow bills, while those of young birds are dark. An excellent and manoeuvrable flyer which is easily identified by its angular wings and forked tail. This opportunistic feeder will prey on various small animals, eat road kills and even steal prey from other raptors.

Food	Nest	Active Period
	1-4	

Habitat	Sociability	Migration

Ulrich Oberprieler (2)

Ad

Imm

African Fish-Eagle
Haliaeetus vocifer 148
Visarend
A large, well-known raptor that is characteristic of the Park's water bodies. Very young birds are mostly brown and gradually acquire the adult plumage over four to five years. Catches fish by swooping down with the feet thrown forward to grasp its prey. The ringing, far-carrying call is often heard. Usually occurs in pairs.

Food	Nest	Active Period
	1-3	

Habitat	Sociability	Migration

Christo Joubert

Secretarybird
Sagittarius serpentarius 118
Sekretarisvoël
A very large, unmistakable raptor. The very long legs and central tail feathers are diagnostic, as is the long droopy crest on the nape. The face is bright orange in adults and yellowish in immatures. Seldom flies; it strides slowly across the veld foraging for prey on the ground. Feeds on a variety of small animals, not only snakes.

Food	Nest	Active Period
	1-3	

Habitat	Sociability	Migration

Lizard Buzzard
Kaupifalco monogrammicus 154
Akkedisvalk

Larger than a dove. It differs from the similar Gabar Goshawk in that it has a black line down the centre of the white throat and one (rarely two) white tail-bar. The belly is finely barred. The white rump may be seen in flight. It hunts ground-living prey from a perch in a tree where it is easily overlooked. Prefers broad-leaved woodland.

Food	Nest	Active Period
	1-3	

Habitat	Sociability	Migration

Lizeth Cillié

Gabar Goshawk
Melierax gabar 161
Witkruissperwer

Larger than a dove. May be confused with the similar-sized Lizard Buzzard (see text of that species). Both adult and immature are similar to the Dark Chanting Goshawk, but are smaller and more compact (see text of that species). Some individuals have a black plumage. The immature is brown, with a streaked chest and a barred belly.

Food	Nest	Active Period
	2-3	

Habitat	Sociability	Migration

Ad

Imm

Burger Cillié (2)

Dark Chanting Goshawk
Melierax metabates 163
Donkersingvalk

This crow-sized bird may be confused with the much smaller Gabar Goshawk, which has a white rump and pale bars on the tail. The immature is most easily distinguished from the immature Gabar Goshawk by its larger size, longer legs and distinctive body shape. Perches conspicuously in trees. Hunts from a perch or while walking on the ground.

Food	Nest	Active Period
	1-2	

Habitat	Sociability	Migration

Ad

Imm

Burger Cillié

Niel Cillié

Ad

Niel Cillié

Imm

Burger Cillié

African Harrier-Hawk
(Gymnogene)
Polyboroides typus 169
Kaalwangvalk
This fairly large raptor is mostly grey with a barred belly, a small elongated head and a bare yellow face, which blushes red with excitement. In flight the black tail has a broad white bar. The immature is brown with a yellow cere and legs. Occurs mainly along riverine habitats. Frequents dead trees in search of prey.

Food	Nest	Active Period
	1-2	
Habitat	Sociability	Migration

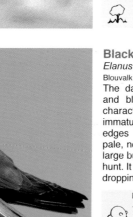

Ad

Christo Joubert

Imm

Burger Cillié

Black-shouldered Kite
Elanus caeruleus 127
Blouvalk
The dark grey back, white underparts and black patches on the shoulders characterise this small raptor. The immature is buffy on the back with pale edges to the feathers. The eyes are pale, not red. Perches conspicuously on large bushes and trees from where it will hunt. It frequently hovers in the air before dropping onto prey.

Food	Nest	Active Period
	2-6	
Habitat	Sociability	Migration

White-backed Vulture
Gyps africanus 123
Witrugaasvoël
The conspicuous white lower back of this vulture can only be seen in flight or when the bird spreads its wings. The rest of the body is brown. The face and eyes are dark. The immature bird is darker and streaked. It is the most common vulture species in the Park and abundant at carcasses. May be confused with the rare Cape Vulture.

Ad

Burger Cillié (2)

Imm

Food	Nest	Active Period
	1	
Habitat	Sociability	Migration

Hooded Vulture
Necrosyrtes monachus 121
Monnikaasvoël

The smallest of the three dark vulture species. The adult has white downy feathers on the back of the head and neck, and the face is pinkish. In the immature these downy feathers are dark brown and the face is brownish. This slender-billed vulture cannot compete with other vultures at carcasses and will pick up scraps. Also eats insects.

Food	Nest	Active Period
	1	

Habitat	Sociability	Migration

Ad

Imm

Burger Cillié (2)

Lappet-faced Vulture
Aegypius tracheliotus 124
Swartaasvoël

This is a huge, dark vulture with a bare, pinkish-red head. It has a large, heavy bill that is used to tear through the skin and tough parts of a carcass. The adult has white feathers on the legs, while those of the immature are brown. Not numerous, but dominates the other vultures at a carcass. Like all the Park's vultures, it nests in trees.

Food	Nest	Active Period
	1	

Habitat	Sociability	Migration

Ad

Imm

Burger Cillié (2)

White-headed Vulture
Aegypius occipitalis 125
Witkopaasvoël

This large vulture is mainly black with a white belly, whitish down on the head and a pink face. The bill is red with a blue cere. The immature has brown underparts and brown down on the head. Usually the first to arrive at a carcass, but it cannot compete with other vultures as they arrive. Sometimes steals food from other large raptors.

Food	Nest	Active Period
	1	

Habitat	Sociability	Migration

Ad

Imm

Ulrich Oberprieler

Burger Cillié

Fruiteaters

The Park's fruiteaters are represented by the mousebirds, turacos (louries), green-pigeons parrots, barbets and tinkerbirds (tinker barbets). All of them have relatively large bills to deal with fruit and berries.

The mousebirds are small grey birds with long tails. They usually occur in flocks and clamber around in trees and bushes in search of food. They superficially resemble the Grey Go-away-bird (a turaco), but are much smaller. Whereas the Grey Go-away-bird is widespread in the Park, the Purple-crested Turaco is confined to denser woodland and riverine growth.

Unlike other pigeons and doves, the African Green-Pigeon is a fruiteater. It may be mistaken for a parrot because of its green plumage and habit of climbing around in fruit-bearing trees. Three parrots occur in the Park. The Brown-headed Parrot is the most widespread, the Grey-headed Parrot occurs mainly in the north, while Meyer's Parrot may be found in the far northern regions.

Barbets and tinkerbirds are small colourful birds that breed in self-excavated holes in trees. They have characteristic far-carrying calls that are often heard. They supplement their diet by feeding on insects.

Burger Cillié

Speckled Mousebird
Colius striatus 424
Gevlekte Muisvoël
This small bird differs from the Red-faced Mousebird in that it is darker, has a blackish face and dark legs. The upper jaw of the bill is black and the lower jaw white. Roost in compact groups at night and on cool days to keep warm. Clambers mouse-like in trees to forage. Flocks fly in a follow-my-leader fashion from tree to tree, i.e. one after the other.

Food	Nest	Active Period
	1-7	
Habitat	Sociability	Migration

Ulrich Oberprieler

Red-faced Mousebird
Urocolius indicus 426
Rooiwangmuisvoël
A small bird. The bare red face and blue eyes of this mousebird are characteristic. Appears more blue-grey than the Speckled Mousebird. It is much more wary than other mousebirds. Compact flocks fly fast and direct from one feeding place to another. Like other mousebirds, it loves to dust-bath. Common in the Park.

Food	Nest	Active Period
	1-7	
Habitat	Sociability	Migration

Purple-crested Turaco
(Purple-crested Lourie)
Gallirex porphyreolophus 371
Bloukuifloerie

Larger than a dove. It has a characteristic dark purple crest and a dark bill. The upperparts are a glossy bluish purple, the chest and neck orange-yellow. The conspicuous dark red flight feathers are only visible in flight. Prefers moist, dense bushveld where it runs along branches. Utters a raucous call.

Food	Nest	Active Period
	1-4	
Habitat	**Sociability**	**Migration**

Niel Cillié

Grey Go-away-bird
(Grey Lourie)
Corythaixoides concolor 373
Kwêvoël

Much larger than the mousebirds. This uniform grey bird with its long tail and crest is a familiar sight in the bushveld. Very noisy, especially when disturbed. The characteristic "kwee-h" and "go-away" calls are easily recognised. May gather at water-points to drink or bath. Often perches on a tree top.

Food	Nest	Active Period
	1-4	
Habitat	**Sociability**	**Migration**

Ulrich Oberprieler

African Green-Pigeon
Treron calvus 361
Papegaaiduif

This large parrot-like pigeon is well camouflaged in leafy trees, due to its green and grey colouration. The legs are red, but the leg feathers are yellow. The two-toned bill is red at the base and white at the tip. Forages in fruit-bearing trees, and often hangs upside down from branches. Usually found in small flocks. Inconspicuous.

Food	Nest	Active Period
	1-2	
Habitat	**Sociability**	**Migration**

Ulrich Oberprieler

Fruiteaters

Brown-headed Parrot
Poicephalus cryptoxanthus 363
Bruinkoppapegaai
Dove-sized. The grey-brown head and neck contrast with the pale green body. It lacks the red shoulder-patches of the larger Grey-headed Parrot. The bright yellow underwings are visible in flight. They occur in small noisy flocks, but are difficult to see in leafy fruit-bearing trees. They fly fast and straight. Drink daily. Often seen in the rest camps.

Food	Nest	Active Period
	2-3	
Habitat	Sociability	Migration

Grey-headed Parrot
Poicephalus fuscicollis suahelicus 362b
Savannepapegaai
This large, mainly green parrot has a grey head and a massive bill. The red forehead, shoulder patches and thighs distinguish it from the Brown-headed Parrot. Prefers woodland with large emergent trees or riverine forest in the northern parts of the Park. It is most common around Punda Maria and Pafuri.

Food	Nest	Active Period
	2-4	
Habitat	Sociability	Migration

Black-collared Barbet
Lybius torquatus 464
Rooikophoutkapper
Smaller than a dove. This barbet has an unmistakable bright red face and throat with a black collar. It has a large black bill and red eyes. The immature's face is a paler orange-red. Excavate their own nests. Roost communally in hollow tree trunks; roosting holes may be used for several years. Very vocal; male and female call in a loud duet.

Food	Nest	Active Period
	2-5	
Habitat	Sociability	Migration

Niel Cillié

Ulrich Oberprieler

Niel Cillié

Crested Barbet
Trachyphonus vaillantii 473
Kuifkophoutkapper
Smaller than a dove. This barbet has a shaggy black crest. The back, tail and broad chest-band are black with white spots. The head, face and belly are yellow with red streaks. A common bird seen in most rest camps. Its call is the well-known "krrrrrrrrrrrrrrrr" sound resembling an alarm clock. It often forages on the ground.

Food	Nest	Active Period
	 1-5	

Habitat	Sociability	Migration

Niel Cillié

Acacia Pied Barbet
Tricholaema leucomelas 465
Bonthoutkapper
Sparrow-sized. The red forehead, yellow eyebrow extending into a white band, and black band through the eyes are characteristic. It has a black throat and white chest. The immature bird has a black forehead. The call resembles that of the African Hoopoe: a soft "hoop" repeated up to 20 times. Also utters a nasal call.

Food	Nest	Active Period
	 2-4	

Habitat	Sociability	Migration

Burger Cillié

Yellow-fronted Tinkerbird
(Yellow-fronted Tinker Barbet)
Pogoniulus chrysoconus 470
Geelblestinker
Smaller than a sparrow. The yellow forehead (sometimes orange) and pale yellow underparts are characteristic. The larger Acacia Pied Barbet has a black throat, white underparts and a red forehead. More often heard than seen; the call is a monotonous but far-carrying "poop, poop, poop".

Food	Nest	Active Period
	 2-3	

Habitat	Sociability	Migration

Niel Cillié

65

Birds with Long Straight Bills

Unlike the birds in previous groups, the birds in this group are smallish (pigeon-sized and smaller) and have short legs. These are the kingfishers and woodpeckers.

The kingfishers are conspicuously coloured birds. Most are waterbirds that usually sit on overhanging reeds or branches, diving into the water to catch fish or other small aquatic animals. A number of African kingfishers, however, are not associated with water at all. They catch insects or other small animals.

Woodpeckers use their bills to chisel away wood in search of insects. Their unique toes and sharp claws enable them to cling to the bark of trees, while the stiff tail-feathers also support their bodies. Woodpeckers are not easily identified, not only because the various species have a similar appearance, but also because the male and female differ from each other. They usually keep close to the trunk of a tree while foraging. Woodpeckers breed in self-excavated tree holes.

Clem Haagner

African Pygmy-Kingfisher
Ispidina picta **432**
Afrikaanse Dwergvisvanger
This is the smallest kingfisher in the region; about sparrow-sized. It has a red bill, broad orange eyebrows and purple ear-patches. The immature has a black bill. This bushveld bird is normally found away from water. Easily overlooked. It perches low on branches and swoops down to catch its insect prey on the ground.

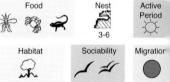

Food	Nest	Active Period
	3-6	

Habitat	Sociability	Migration

Burger Cillié

Malachite Kingfisher
Alcedo cristata **431**
Kuifkopvisvanger
A very small kingfisher (sparrow-sized) with a red bill, blue upperparts and orange-brown underparts. May be confused with the African Pygmy-Kingfisher but lacks the orange eyebrow and purple ear patches. The immature has a black bill. It perches motionless, peering into the water and dives for prey. It flies fast and low over the water.

Food	Nest	Active Period
	3-6	

Habitat	Sociability	Migration

66

Woodland Kingfisher
Halcyon senegalensis 433
Bosveldvisvanger
Smaller than a dove. This kingfisher has turquoise upperparts and a white belly. The bill is red above and black below. The black stripe through the eye is characteristic. On the wings are large black patches. Occurs in wooded areas throughout the Park where its charac- teristic loud "kri-tirrrrrr" sound is often heard.

Food	Nest	Active Period
	2-4	

Habitat	Sociability	Migration

Brown-hooded Kingfisher
Halcyon albiventris 435
Bruinkopvisvanger
Smaller than a dove. The brown, streaked head and red bill with a black tip are diagnostic. In the male the upper back is black and in the female it is brown. The wings, tail and rump are blue and more visible in flight. Found throughout the Park, usually in bushveld away from water. It hunts insects from a perch. The characteristic call is often heard.

Food	Nest	Active Period
	2-5	

Habitat	Sociability	Migration

Striped Kingfisher
Halcyon chelicuti 437
Gestreepte Visvanger
Smaller than a dove. The dark, streaked cap, the dark band through the eyes and the white collar are characteristic. The bill is black above and red below. The extensive white patches on the underwing are visible in flight. Found away from water in a variety of wooded habitats. Perches low in trees. Unobtrusive.

Food	Nest	Active Period
	2-6	

Habitat	Sociability	Migration

Burger Cillié

Niel Cillié

Ulrich Oberprieler

Ulrich Oberprieler

67

Birds with Long Straight Bills

Pied Kingfisher
Ceryle rudis 428
Bontvisvanger
Dove-sized. The only black-and-white kingfisher in the region. The male and female differ in that the male has a second, narrower black band across the chest. It hunts from a perch or hovers above the water before diving for aquatic prey. Fish are usually battered to death before being swallowed head-first. Bold and tame.

Food	Nest	Active Period
	2-6	
Habitat	**Sociability**	**Migration**

Giant Kingfisher
Megaceryle maximus 429
Reusevisvanger
The largest kingfisher in the Park; larger than a dove. Unmistakable. It has a long heavy black bill and spotted upperparts. The male has a brown chest and a black belly with white spots. In the female these colours are reversed. Perches on branches overhanging water and is easily overlooked unless calling loudly. Catches mostly crabs and frogs.

Food	Nest	Active Period
	2-6	
Habitat	**Sociability**	**Migration**

Cardinal Woodpecker
Dendropicos fuscescens 486
Kardinaalspeg
A small woodpecker with a short bill, black moustachial stripes and a brown forecrown. In the male the hindcrown is red while the female's is black. The back is barred, and the chest is streaked. When disturbed, it hops out of view behind a tree trunk. Often drums its bill against a hollow branch. Roosts in a tree hole at night.

Food	Nest	Active Period
	1-5	
Habitat	**Sociability**	**Migration**

Bennett's Woodpecker
Campethera bennettii 481
Bennettse Speg

Larger than a sparrow. It differs from the Golden-tailed Woodpecker in that the back is barred and the underparts are spotted. The male has a red crown and moustachial stripes. In the female the stripe below the eyes is brown, and only the hindcrown is red. Forages on the ground more often than other woodpeckers, feeding on ants and termites.

Food	Nest	Active Period
	2-4	
Habitat	Sociability	Migration

Golden-tailed Woodpecker
Campethera abingoni 483
Goudstertspeg

Larger than a sparrow. The streaked underparts are the main difference between this woodpecker and Bennett's Woodpecker. In the male the forecrown is mottled black on red, and the hindcrown and moustachial stripe are red. The female has a spotted, black forecrown and red hindcrown. It forages in trees for insects.

Food	Nest	Active Period
	2-4	
Habitat	Sociability	Migration

Bearded Woodpecker
Dendropicos namaquus 487
Baardspeg

A large woodpecker with a long bill. The black moustachial stripes and ear coverts are conspicuous. The forecrown is spotted white on black; the male has a red hindcrown while the female's is black. The underparts are barred. The loud drumming sound of its bill against dead wood is an indication of its presence.

Food	Nest	Active Period
	2-4	
Habitat	Sociability	Migration

69

Birds with Long Decurved Bills

Although some birds in previous groups may also have long, decurved bills, the birds in this group are all crow-sized or smaller (except the Southern Ground-Hornbill), and have short legs.

Hornbills are characterised by their robust bills, which are often enlarged by a horny ridge on top, especially in the males. The colour and the specific size of the bill are a good guide to identify the species.

The African Hoopoe is a conspicuous and well-known bird that usually forages on the ground, while the Green Wood-Hoopoe and Greater Scimitarbill look for insects in trees.

The colourful bee-eaters catch bees and other insects in flight, and then return to a perch to eat them. These agile fliers are characterised by their triangular, pointed wings.

The sunbirds feed on nectar and are thus associated with nectar-producing flowers. The iridescent, glossy colours render the males very conspicuous, while most females (and non-breeding males of some species) are dully coloured and near-impossible to identify.

Southern Ground-Hornbill
Bucorvus leadbeateri 463
Bromvoël
An unmistakable, large turkey-like black bird with a very large bill. In adults the bare face and inflatable throat skin are red, in immatures yellowish-orange. Females have a blue patch on the throat. The white flight-feathers are visible in flight, but these birds are reluctant fliers. They walk along slowly in search of food. The call is deep and booming.

Food	Nest	Active Period
	1-2	

Habitat	Sociability	Migration

Trumpeter Hornbill
Bycanistes bucinator 455
Gewone Boskraai
This large hornbill is mainly black with a white rump, belly and underwings. The large pointed casque on the upper jaw and the bare red facial skin are diagnostic. The female has a smaller bill and a much reduced casque. Conspicuous and noisy; the call sounds like a baby crying. Prefers riverine woodland and forages mainly in trees.

Food	Nest	Active Period
	2-4	

Habitat	Sociability	Migration

African Grey Hornbill
Tockus nasutus 457
Grysneushoringvoël
Grey, with whitish underparts. The male has a dark grey bill with a creamy stripe at the base and a large casque. The female has a smaller, pale yellow bill with a red tip and a smaller casque. Its presence is revealed by high-pitched whistling calls. Forages in trees and will catch insects fleeing from veld fires. A conspicuous bird.

Food	Nest	Active Period
	3-5	
Habitat	Sociability	Migration

Southern Yellow-billed Hornbill
Tockus leucomelas 459
Suidelike Geelbekneushoringvoël
The large yellow bill distinguishes it from the other hornbills. The eyes are yellow and the facial skin pink. Forages mainly on the ground. The call is similar to, but slightly lower-toned, than that of the Red-billed Hornbill. Like other hornbills, the female is sealed into the nest hollow when breeding, leaving only a narrow slit through which the male feeds her.

Food	Nest	Active Period
	3-5	
Habitat	Sociability	Migration

Red-billed Hornbill
Tockus erythrorhynchus 458
Rooibekneushoringvoël
It has a characteristic slender red bill. The back and wings are blotched black and white. The underparts are white. Forages on the ground by digging in the soil or in dung. Like the Southern Yellow-billed Hornbill, it displays by bobbing up and down with a bowed head. The male feeds the female through a slit in the enclosed nest during breeding.

Food	Nest	Active Period
	3-7	
Habitat	Sociability	Migration

African Hoopoe
Upupa africana 451
Hoephoep
A well-known, dove-sized, cinnamon coloured bird with a long decurved bill and a long black-tipped crest. The wings and back are black with white bands. The pointed crest may be raised when the bird is alarmed. This common bird is very tame in some rest camps. It forages on the ground, probing into the soil with its bill in search of insects.

Food	Nest	Active Period
	 2-6	

Habitat	Sociability	Migration

Ad

Imm

Green Wood-Hoopoe
(Red-billed Wood-Hoopoe)
Phoeniculus purpureus 452
Rooibekkakelaar
This dove-sized wood-hoopoe differs from the smaller Common Scimitarbill in that it has a red, less decurved bill and red legs. It appears dark at a distance, but the head and upperparts are iridescent blue-green. The immature has a black bill. Active noisy birds. Forage by probing loose bark in search of insects.

Food	Nest	Active Period
	 2-5	

Habitat	Sociability	Migration

Common Scimitarbill
(Scimitar-billed Wood-Hoopoe)
Rhinopomastus cyanomelas 454
Swartbekkakelaar
The black legs and feet, as well as the extremely decurved, thin black bill distinguish it from the larger Green Wood-Hoopoe and its juveniles which have black bills. A white bar on the outer primaries is visible in flight. It forages on the outer branches of trees and sometimes on the ground.

Food	Nest	Active Period
	 2-4	

Habitat	Sociability	Migration

European Bee-eater
Merops apiaster **438**
Europese Byvreter

Slightly smaller than a dove. This is the only bee-eater with a chestnut crown and upper wings. The yellow throat is separated by a black collar from the blue underparts. These birds arrive in the Park during early summer. Large flocks often fly high up in the air, calling continuously. Roost in tall trees at night. They hunt insects in flight.

Food	Nest	Active Period
	EURASIA 2-6	

Habitat	Sociability	Migration

Willemien Cillié

Southern Carmine Bee-eater
Merops nubicoides **441**
Suidelike Rooiborsbyvreter

About dove-sized. A very attractive bee-eater with its overall red colour and elongated central tail-feathers. It has a turquoise crown and pale blue vent and rump. The immature is duller and lacks the long central tail feathers. It forages in the air and is attracted to veld fires, feeding on fleeing insects. More common in the southern parts.

Food	Nest	Active Period
	AFRICA	

Habitat	Sociability	Migration

Ulrich Oberprieler

White-fronted Bee-eater
Merops bullockoides **443**
Rooikeelbyvreter

Smaller than a dove. A very colourful bird with a characteristic red throat and a white forehead and chin. The wings and tail are green, the vent and rump bright blue and the crown and chest cinnamon. They are associated with rivers where they breed in colonies in riverbanks. They hunt from a perch, in the air or over water.

Food	Nest	Active Period
	2-5	

Habitat	Sociability	Migration

Burger Cillié

Ad

Imm

Ulrich Oberprieler

Niel Cillié

Little Bee-eater
Merops pusillus 444

Kleinbyvreter

The smallest bee-eater in the region: slightly larger than a sparrow. It has green upperparts with a turquoise eyebrow and a vivid yellow throat with a black border. The immature lacks the black border on the throat. Roosts in thickets, usually near rivers. Prefers open areas where it hunts from a low perch.

Food	Nest	Active Period
	2-6	

Habitat	Sociability	Migration

♂

♀

Niel Cillié (2)

Collared Sunbird
Hedydipna collaris 793

Kortbeksuikerbekkie

This very small sunbird has a much shorter bill than other sunbirds. The male has a glossy green head and upperparts, bright yellow underparts with a narrow blue-purple chest-band. The female is uniform yellow below, without the chest-band. Often seen foraging in flowering creepers. Uses its short bill to slit the base of flowers.

Food	Nest	Active Period
	1-4	

Habitat	Sociability	Migration

♂

♀

Niel Cillié (2)

White-bellied Sunbird
Cinnyris talatala 787

Witpenssuikerbekkie

Smaller than a sparrow. The male's metallic green head, throat and upperparts, the glossy purple chestband and white belly are diagnostic. The female is grey-brown with off-white underparts. A highly vocal and restless bird, it is always coming and going. Males sing from the topmost branches of a tree during the breeding season.

Food	Nest	Active Period
	1-3	

Habitat	Sociability	Migration

Birds with Long Decurved Bills

Marico Sunbird
Cinnyris mariquensis 779
Maricosuikerbekkie
About sparrow-sized. The male's head, throat and upperparts are iridescent green and a wide purple chest-band separates the green throat from the black belly. The female is olive-grey with brown streaks on the throat and chest. It is an active bird. Aggressive towards other sunbirds. A very common sunbird that occurs mainly in thornveld.

Food	Nest	Active Period
	2	

Habitat	Sociability	Migration

♂ ♀

Scarlet-chested Sunbird
Chalcomitra senegalensis 791
Rooiborssuikerbekkie
About sparrow-sized. The male is unmistakable: black with a bright scarlet throat and chest. It has a glossy green forecrown and chin. The female is grey above and the underparts are olive-yellow with darker blotches. The male is very vocal and aggressive towards other sunbirds and will chase them away. Often seen in the rest camps.

Food	Nest	Active Period
	1-3	

Habitat	Sociability	Migration

♂ ♀

Amethyst Sunbird
(African Black Sunbird)
Chalcomitra amethystina 792
Swartsuikerbekkie
About sparrow-sized. The male looks black from a distance, but in bright sunlight the metallic purple throat and glossy green forecrown are visible. The female is pale grey with streaked underparts. She is not as heavily blotched as the female Scarlet-chested Sunbird. Occurs in higher-lying areas.

Food	Nest	Active Period
	1-3	

Habitat	Sociability	Migration

♂ ♀

75

Aerial Insectivores

The long slender wings enable these birds to catch insects in flight. They are thus excellent fliers with small triangular bills.

The nightjars are roughly dove-sized birds. Their characteristic calls are often heard at night. During the day they perch on the ground (rarely in trees), where their camouflaging colours make them nearly invisible and very difficult to identify.

Swallows are often confused with swifts. Swallows (and the closely related martins) have angular wings that are easily recognised in flight. Their toes enable them to grip and they are thus often seen perched on branches or wires.

Swifts (and the closely related spinetails) on the other hand, have sickle-shaped wings. They are usually seen in flight as their four small, forward-pointing toes only enable them to cling to vertical surfaces such as cliffs or walls: they are unable to perch like swallows. As all the swifts are dully coloured and difficult to identify, only one species is described in this guide.

Ulrich Oberprieler

Rufous-cheeked Nightjar
Caprimulgus rufigena **406**
Rooiwangnaguil
Nightjars are dove-sized nocturnal birds. During the day they roost on the ground where their brown colour camouflages them well. This nightjar is best identified by its call which is often heard during spring and summer: a number of "awok" sounds followed by a drawn-out "prrrrrrrrrrrrrrrrrrr" sounding like a small engine. Breeds on the ground.

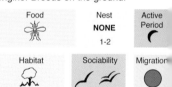

Food	Nest	Active Period
🦟	NONE	(
	1-2	

Habitat	Sociability	Migration
🌳	✓ 🕊	●

Burger Cillié

Fiery-necked Nightjar
Caprimulgus pectoralis **405**
Afrikaanse Naguil
This dove-sized bird roosts under a bush or in thickets during the day. At night it hunts insects in flight. It is the most common and widespread nightjar in the Park. The characteristic call indicates its presence: it starts with an up-and-down whistle and ends with trilling notes falling in tone, sounding like "good lord, deliver us". Breeds on the ground.

Food	Nest	Active Period
🦟	NONE	(
	1-2	

Habitat	Sociability	Migration
🌳	✓ 🕊	○

76

Barn Swallow
(European Swallow)
Hirundo rustica 518
Europese Swael

It differs from the Wire-tailed Swallow in that it has a rufous forehead and throat with a broad dark chest-band. The deeply forked tail, white underparts and metallic blue-black upperparts are other characteristics. Visits the Park during summer. Often seen hunting insects over grassy patches.

Food	Nest	Active Period
	EUROPE	

Habitat	Sociability	Migration

Niel Cillié

Red-breasted Swallow
Hirundo semirufa 524
Rooiborsswael

A large swallow. The upperparts, including the cheeks, are a dark metallic blue, while the underparts and underwing coverts are a deep chestnut. The tail is deeply forked. (The similar Mosque Swallow, found mainly in the northern parts of the Park, has a white throat, cheeks and underwing coverts.) The nest is a bowl with a tunnel entrance.

Food	Nest	Active Period
	UNIQUE 3	

Habitat	Sociability	Migration

Burger Cillié

Wire-tailed Swallow
Hirundo smithii 522
Draadstertswael

The chestnut cap, white underparts and blue-black upperparts are characteristic. A black vent-band is seen in flight. The forked tail has two extremely thin tail streamers, hence the name. Always associated with water. Often perches on bridges, power lines and railings. It forages for insects in the air. The nest is a half-cup built of mud.

Food	Nest	Active Period
	UNIQUE 2-3	

Habitat	Sociability	Migration

Niel Cillié

77

Greater Striped Swallow
Hirundo cucullata 526
Grootstreepswael

It differs from the Lesser Striped Swallow in that it is larger, has white ear-coverts and finely streaked underparts, which may not be visible in flight. The crown and rump are chestnut and the upperparts are metallic blue-black. Forages over open grassland and water. Builds a ball-shaped nest of mud with a tunnel entrance.

Food	Nest	Active Period
	**UNIQUE** 2-4	

Habitat	Sociability	Migration

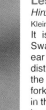

Lesser Striped Swallow
Hirundo abyssinica 527
Kleinstreepswael

It is smaller than the Greater Striped Swallow. The crown, hind neck and ear coverts are deep chestnut. May be distinguished by the very bold streaks on the white underparts. The tail is deeply forked. It is a common breeding resident in the Park. Highly vocal, it often perches in a prominent place. The nest is a mud bowl with a tunnel entrance.

Food	Nest	Active Period
	UNIQUE 2-4	

Habitat	Sociability	Migration

Little Swift
Apus affinis 417
Kleinwindswael

This small dark swift has a white throat, a broad white rump and a square tail which may look rounded in flight. (The similar White-rumped Swift has a narrow white rump and a deeply forked tail.) A very common bird that may be seen in large flocks. Continuously twitters in flight. Builds it cup-shaped nest under bridges. Breeds in colonies.

Food	Nest	Active Period
	UNIQUE 2-3	

Habitat	Sociability	Migration

The upper jaw of a typical insectivore's bill is slightly decurved or even hooked at the tip. Although most of the birds in this group feed primarily on insects, they may also take other small animals, and the crows even feed on carrion.

The Pied Crow is most likely to be seen anywhere in the Park, while the Cape Crow and White-necked Raven may rarely be seen in the north. The characteristically coloured coucals usually creep through dense aquatic vegetation and are more often heard than seen.

The rollers are bluish or purple, dove-sized birds. They perch quietly for long periods, then flying to catch insects in the air or on the ground. They are noisy during the breeding season and display in a typical rolling, tumbling fashion.

A large variety of shrikes occur in different habitats throughout the Park. The bush-shrikes are brightly coloured, especially on the underparts and have far-carrying calls. The tchagras have brown backs and rufous wings, while the boubous have pale underparts and a white wingstripe on the black upperparts.

Pied Crow
Corvus albus 548
Witborskraai
This well known crow is characterised by its white belly and collar. The rest of the bird is shiny black. The immature is a slightly duller version of the adult. It forages mainly on the ground by walking, but hops when moving fast. Often seen in flight. Mainly a scavenger, it will eat almost anything. It roosts in trees or on poles. Utters a harsh, deep croak.

Food	Nest	Active Period
	1-7	

Habitat	Sociability	Migration

Burger Cillié

Burchell's Coucal
Centropus burchellii 391
Gewone Vleiloerie
Larger than a dove, with a long, broad tail. An unmistakable bird with a dark head and tail, chestnut upperparts and creamy-white underparts. The long tail is barred at the base. The immature has a brown head, a white eyebrow and white streaks on the nape. Shy and secretive. Forages in dense vegetation. The bubbling call is often heard.

Food	Nest	Active Period
	2-5	

Habitat	Sociability	Migration

Ad

Imm

Burger Cillié (2)

Insectivores with Stout Bills

European Roller
Coracias garrulus 446
Europese Troupant

About dove-sized. Unlike the Lilac breasted Roller, this roller has a square tail. It is mainly blue with brown upperparts. During the height of summer this is the most common roller in the Park. It usually hunts from a perch and glides down to catch prey. Is attracted to veld fires and locust swarms. Normally silent.

Food	Nest	Active Period
	EURASIA	

Habitat	Sociability	Migration
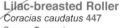		

Lilac-breasted Roller
Coracias caudatus 447
Gewone Troupant

About dove-sized. A very colourful roller. The blue underparts and lilac chest are diagnostic, as are the long tail-streamers which are, however, absent in the duller immature bird. (The similar Racket-tailed Roller may be seen in the far north. It lacks the lilac chest.) It is usually seen on a perch, from where it catches its prey. Attracted to grassy areas.

Food	Nest	Active Period
	2-4	

Habitat	Sociability	Migration

Purple Roller
Coracias naevius 449
Groottroupant

Slightly larger than the others, this roller may be identified by the pale eyebrow, heavily streaked, lilac-brown underparts and the square tail. It has a purple rump and tail, but is much duller than the other rollers. It defends its territory aggressively, chasing other birds away. Perches on dead branches. Fairly quiet, its call is loud and rasping.

Food	Nest	Active Period
	2-4	

Habitat	Sociability	Migration

Broad-billed Roller
Eurystomus glaucurus 450
Geelbektroupant
About dove-sized. The bright yellow bill of this dark roller is diagnostic. The throat, chest and belly are purple. The upperparts are cinnamon and the rump and tail blue. It perches high in trees, especially in riverine woodland, flying occasionally to catch prey. It drinks in flight by dipping down to the water. Occurs mainly in the far northern parts.

Food	Nest	Active Period
	2-4	

Habitat	Sociability	Migration

Niel Cillié

Orange-breasted Bush-Shrike
Telophorus sulfureopectus 748
Oranjeborsboslaksman
Smaller than a dove. This colourful shrike may be distinguished from the larger Grey-headed Bush-Shrike by the dark eyes, as well as the yellow eyebrow and forehead. The immature lacks the orange breast of the adult. It prefers thickets and dense bush. More often heard than seen: utters a characteristic "cof-fee-tea-or-meee" whistle.

Food	Nest	Active Period
	1-3	

Habitat	Sociability	Migration

Niel Cillié

Grey-headed Bush-Shrike
Malaconotus blanchoti 751
Spookvoël
This large shrike has a characteristic large black bill and yellow eyes. The head and mantle are grey, the underparts yellow. It lacks the yellow eyebrow and forehead of the smaller Orange-breasted Bush-Shrike. Very secretive and easily overlooked in the lower canopy of trees. The call is a characteristic ghostly, drawn-out "whoooo".

Food	Nest	Active Period
	2-4	

Habitat	Sociability	Migration

Burger Cillié

81

Burger Cillié

Lesser Grey Shrike
Lanius minor 731
Gryslaksman

Smaller than a dove. This shrike has a black forehead, face and ear-coverts. The crown and mantle are grey, which differs from the chestnut upperparts of the male Red-backed Shrike. The underparts are white and the wings have white wing-patches. The immature lacks the black forehead. It hunts from a perch, dropping onto prey on the ground.

Food	Nest	Active Period
	EURASIA	

Habitat	Sociability	Migration

Burger Cillié (2)

Red-backed Shrike
Lanius collurio 733
Rooiruglaksman

Smaller than a dove. The male is easily identifiable. He has a grey crown, a black band through the eye and a chestnut-coloured back. The female and immature are more non-descript: grey-brown upperparts and mottled underparts. A common and conspicuous bird during summer. Forages from a perch and sometimes impales its prey on a thorn.

Food	Nest	Active Period
	EURASIA	

Habitat	Sociability	Migration

Niel Cillié (2)

Black-backed Puffback
Dryoscopus cubla 740
Sneeubal

A small black-and-white shrike with diagnostic red eyes. The male has a black cap on the head, while the female's forehead is white. The name of this bird describes the male's courtship display when he fluffs out the white rump feathers. It forages high in trees where it is easily overlooked, were it not for its characteristic "click-whistle" call.

Food	Nest	Active Period
	2-3	

Habitat	Sociability	Migration

Southern Boubou
Laniarius ferrugineus 736
Suidelike Waterfiskaal

The black upperparts, creamy-rufous underparts and white wing-bar characterise this shrike. (The similar Tropical Boubou only occurs in the far north. Its underparts are off-white.) A very vocal but highly secretive bird, keeping to undergrowth and thickets. A pair often calls a highly variable duet, regularly uttering the characteristic "boo-boo".

Food	Nest	Active Period
	2-3	
Habitat	**Sociability**	**Migration**

Ulrich Oberprieler

Brown-crowned Tchagra
(Three-streaked Tchagra)
Tchagra australis 743
Rooivlerktjagra

Smaller than a dove. Very similar to the Black-crowned Tchagra, but it has a brown crown with black stripes below and above the broad white eyebrow. It forages mainly on the ground in thickets. During courtship the male performs an upward-spiralling aerial display while singing.

Food	Nest	Active Period
	2-4	
Habitat	**Sociability**	**Migration**

Ulrich Oberprieler

Black-crowned Tchagra
Tchagra senegalus 744
Swartkroontjagra

Smaller than a dove. It is slightly larger than the Brown-crowned Tchagra and has a completely black crown and a white eyebrow. The immature has a mottled crown and is duller. It is more arboreal than the Brown-crowned Tchagra, but also forages on the ground. Shy and wary. Sounds like a drunk person whistling on his way home.

Food	Nest	Active Period
	2-4	
Habitat	**Sociability**	**Migration**

Burger Cillié

Insectivores with Stout Bills

Niel Cillié

White-crested Helmet-Shrike
(White Helmet-Shrike)
Prionops plumatus 753
Withelmlaksman
Smaller than a dove. A black-and-white shrike with a grey head. The yellow eyes and eye-wattles are diagnostic. The immature is more brownish and lacks the eye-wattles. Usually found in sociable groups that coordinate their activities by calling. Flies in a butterfly-like fashion from tree to tree.

Food	Nest	Active Period
	2-5	

Habitat	Sociability	Migration

Burger Cillié

Southern White-crowned Shrike
Eurocephalus anguitimens 756
Kremetartlaksman
Unmistakable. The only large shrike with a white crown and forehead. The adult is black and white, while the immature is more brownish. They prefer to forage in small groups. Flocks are very vocal. It usually perches on the top or outer branches of a tree. Usually found in acacia woodland with an open understorey.

Food	Nest	Active Period
	2-5	

Habitat	Sociability	Migration

Magpie Shrike
(African Long-tailed Shrike)
Corvinella melanoleuca 735
Langstertlaksman
The only shrike with an extremely long tail. It is mainly black with a white "V" on the lower back. The female has white patches on the flanks. In flight the white patches on the wings are conspicuous. It flies fast and quite low over short distances, swooping upwards to perch. Utters a characteristic whistle.

Food	Nest	Active Period
	2-6	

Habitat	Sociability	Migration

Burger Cillié

84

A large variety of birds belong to this group. Although all of them have the decurved upper jaw of a typical insectivore, some species also feed on fruit or even seeds and nectar.

The cuckoos are characterised by their monotonous calls: they are more often heard than seen. All of them are migratory and visit the Park in spring and summer. The bright yellow colours make the orioles very conspicuous. Just like the bulbuls and greenbuls they also feed on fruit. Babblers are group-living, noisy birds. They superficially resemble the thrushes. The robin-chats and scrub-robins are well known for their beautiful song. They forage on the ground in dense vegetation. Most flycatchers catch insects in flight. They are quiet, gentle birds. The batises are small, characteristically coloured shrikes.

Larks, pipits and longclaws are ground-living, well-camouflaged birds. Their identification is facilitated by listening to their characteristic calls. Wagtails usually occur near water while ox-peckers are associated with larger game on which they look for ticks and other parasites. The plumage of the omnivorous starlings is glossy and iridescent, the colour changing according to light conditions.

African Cuckoo
Cuculus gularis 375
Afrikaanse Koekoek

About dove-sized. The upperparts are grey, while the white underparts are barred. It differs from the Common Cuckoo (a summer visitor) in that the undertail is barred, not spotted. The diagnostic "hoop-hoop" call is more drawn out than that of the African Hoopoe. It is a very shy and secretive bird. A brood parasite of the Fork-tailed Drongo.

Food	Nest	Active Period
	BREEDING PARASITE	
Habitat	Sociability	Migration

Niel Cillié

Red-chested Cuckoo
Cuculus solitarius 377
Piet-my-vrou

About dove-sized. The rufous chest and dark eyes distinguish it from the African and Common Cuckoos. A secretive bird that perches high in trees. Very vocal in spring. The male's call gave rise to the Afrikaans name "Piet-my-vrou", which is repeated monotonously, even at night. A brood parasite of mostly robins and thrushes.

Food	Nest	Active Period
	BREEDING PARASITE	
Habitat	Sociability	Migration

Burger Cillié

♂

♀

Burger Cillié

Ulrich Oberprieler

Diderick Cuckoo
Chrysococcyx caprius 386
Diederikkie
Larger than a sparrow. The upperparts of the male are metallic green (more coppery in the female). The red eyes, white spots on the wings and heavily barred flanks are diagnostic. The immature is unique in that it has a red bill. The male calls a persistent "dee-dee-deederick" for extended periods. Brood parasitises weavers and sparrows.

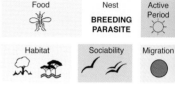

Food	Nest	Active Period
	BREEDING PARASITE	

Habitat	Sociability	Migration

♂

♀

Niel Cillié (2)

Klaas's Cuckoo
Chrysococcyx klaas 385
Meitjie
Larger than a sparrow. The male differs from the Diderick Cuckoo in that it has dark eyes and lacks the white spots on the wing and the bold barring on the flanks. The female appears more coppery above, with fine barring on both the upperparts and flanks. A shy bird. The call is a whistled "mhee-ki", hence the Afrikaans name. Brood parasitises various birds.

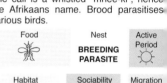

Food	Nest	Active Period
	BREEDING PARASITE	

Habitat	Sociability	Migration

Burger Cillié

Jacobin Cuckoo
Clamator jacobinus 382
Bontnuwejaarsvoël
Larger than a dove. It has black upperparts, white underparts, a crested head and white patches on the primaries. The similar Levaillant's (Striped) Cuckoo has stripes on its throat. A black form is similar to the Black Cuckoo, except for the crested head. Brood parasitises mainly the Dark-capped Bulbul.

Food	Nest	Active Period
	BREEDING PARASITE	

Habitat	Sociability	Migration

Fork-tailed Drongo
Dicrurus adsimilis 541
Mikstertbyvanger
Smaller than a dove. This all-black bird has a deeply forked tail. The red eyes may not be seen in bad light conditions. A common bird throughout the Park. It catches prey from an exposed perch in fast flight or on the ground. Mobs large birds of prey and may rob food from other birds. It is very vocal and may mimic calls of other birds.

Food	Nest	Active Period
	  2-4	

Habitat	Sociability	Migration

Burger Cillié

Southern Black Flycatcher
Melaenornis pammelaina 694
Swartvlieëvanger
About sparrow-sized. May be confused with the Fork-tailed Drongo, but is smaller and has a square tail and dark (not red) eyes. This black bird is quiet and prefers to forage in the mid-canopy rather than high up in the open like the Fork-tailed Drongo. It catches insects in flight or on the ground and returns to its perch.

Food	Nest	Active Period
	  3-5	

Habitat	Sociability	Migration

Burger Cillié

Southern Black Tit
Parus niger 554
Gewone Swartmees
About sparrow-sized. This small black bird has conspicuous white markings on the wings. The female is duller and slightly greyer on the belly than the male. It is noisy and chatters continuously while foraging restlessly in trees. Feeds mostly on caterpillars. It may join other birds during the day, but roosts on its own.

Food	Nest	Active Period
	  2-3	

Habitat	Sociability	Migration

Niel Cillié

87

Insectivores with Medium-sized Bills

Black-headed Oriole
Oriolus larvatus 546
Swartkopwielewaal
Smaller than a dove. A strikingly yellow bird with a black head and upper chest. It has a characteristic red bill and red eyes. The immature is much duller with black streaks on the underparts and it has a black bill and eyes. Very vocal: the call is a liquid whistle. A fairly common bird in the Park. Usually feeds in large trees and at aloe flowers during winter.

Food	Nest	Active Period
	2-4	
Habitat	Sociability	Migration

Arrow-marked Babbler
Turdoides jardineii 560
Pylvlekkatlagter
Smaller than a dove. The white arrow-like streaks on the head and chest, and the reddish eyes are diagnostic. The immature has brown eyes and lacks the white markings on the underparts. A common bird in the Park, usually seen in small groups. Forages on or close to the ground. Very vocal: the call resembles that of the Green Wood-Hoopoe.

Food	Nest	Active Period
	2-4	
Habitat	Sociability	Migration

Kurrichane Thrush
Turdus libonyanus 576
Rooibeklyster
Smaller than a dove. The bright orange-red bill, white throat with black malar stripes and the orange-brown flanks are diagnostic. A common resident, it may be seen on the lawns in rest camps and in open woodland. It forages by typically running across open spaces, stopping and pecking at food on the ground. The call is a loud whistle.

Food	Nest	Active Period
	2-4	
Habitat	Sociability	Migration

White-browed Robin-Chat
(Heuglin's Robin)
Cossypha heuglini 599
Heuglinse Janfrederik

Larger than a sparrow. The completely orange underparts and the black head with the conspicuous white eyebrows are characteristic. This shy bird keeps to thickets along rivers or in rest camps and is not easily seen, but it is very vocal with various beautiful song phrases. Forages mainly on the ground.

Food	Nest	Active Period
	2	

Habitat	Sociability	Migration

Burger Cillié

Red-capped Robin-Chat
(Natal Robin)
Cossypha natalensis 600
Nataljanfrederik

Larger than a sparrow. The orange underparts and face distinguish it from other robin-chats. The back and wings are metallic blue-grey, the crown and nape rufous-brown. Secretive. Occurs mostly in thickets along some of the major rivers. Forages on the ground. Imitates a wide variety of sounds.

Food	Nest	Active Period
	2-4	

Habitat	Sociability	Migration

 Niel Cillié

White-throated Robin-Chat
(White-throated Robin)
Cossypha humeralis 602
Witkeeljanfrederik

Larger than a sparrow. The only robin-chat with a white wing-bar, chest and throat. At a quick glance it may be confused with the larger Southern Boubou. A shy bird that keeps to thickets along rivers and other watercourses. It forages on the ground, hopping around actively. The song is melodious.

Food	Nest	Active Period
	2-3	

Habitat	Sociability	Migration

Niel Cillié

89

Insectivores with Medium-sized Bills

White-browed Scrub-Robin
(White-browed Robin)
Cercotrichas leucophrys 613
Gestreepte Wipstert

About sparrow-sized. The heavily streaked chest and white bars on the wing-coverts are characteristic. The rump is rufous. Widespread in the Park. Aggressive towards other birds. It hops on the ground while foraging. Sometimes flicks its tail up and down. Utters a melodious, but repetitive song.

Food	Nest	Active Period
	2-4	

Habitat	Sociability	Migration

Bearded Scrub-Robin
(Eastern Bearded Robin)
Cercotrichas quadrivirgata 617
Baardwipstert

Slightly larger than a sparrow. An attractive scrub-robin, characterised by the orange flanks and chest, the white patches on the wings and the bold malar stripes. Seen mostly in the thickets along the major river coursres where it forages on the ground. The melodious song is often repeated.

Food	Nest	Active Period
	2-3	

Habitat	Sociability	Migration

Groundscraper Thrush
Psophocichla litsitsirupa 580
Gevlekte Lyster

Smaller than a dove. The upperparts are brown-grey and the white underparts are marked with bold black streaks and blotches. It usually stands very upright and has the habit of flicking one wing at a time. Prefers open areas with short grass, like lawns in rest camps. They gather in loose flocks when not breeding. Very conspicuous.

Food	Nest	Active Period
	2-4	

Habitat	Sociability	Migration

Chinspot Batis
Batis molitor 701
Witliesbosbontrokkie

A small black-and-white bird with pale yellow eyes. The female has a dark chestnut chest-band and a chestnut patch on the throat while the male has a black chest-band and a white throat. The descending, three-syllabled call sounds like "three-blind-mice". Widespread and common. It forages actively in the canopy of trees.

Food	Nest	Active Period
	1-4	

Habitat	Sociability	Migration

♂ ♀ Niel Cillié (2)

Mocking Cliff-Chat
(Mocking Chat)
Thamnolaea cinnamomeiventris 593
Dassievoël

Smaller than a dove. The male is glossy black with characteristic white wing-patches. The belly, vent and rump are bright chestnut. The female is dark grey above with a duller chestnut belly and undertail, and lacks the white patches on the wings. Occurs in rocky areas. The call is melodious, including imitations.

Food	Nest	Active Period
	2-4	

Habitat	Sociability	Migration

♂ ♀ Burger Cillié Niel Cillié

African Stonechat
(Common Stonechat)
Saxicola torquatus 596
Gewone Bontrokkie

Sparrow-sized. The male is unmistakable with its black head, white nape, wings and rump, and rufous chest. The female has a pale brown head and upperparts, a cinnamon chest, a white rump and white patches on the wings. Prefers grassy areas where it perches conspicuously. Flicks its wings and tail on landing.

Food	Nest	Active Period
	2-5	

Habitat	Sociability	Migration

♂ ♀ Niel Cillié Burger Cillié

Insectivores with Medium-sized Bills

Dark-capped Bulbul
(Black-eyed Bulbul)
Pycnonotus tricolor **568**
Swartoogtiptol
Larger than a sparrow. It has a slightl
crested black head, black eye-rings
whitish belly and yellow undertail coverts
A common, prominent bird in the Park.
is a restless bird and usually the first to
sound the alarm if there is a snake o
other predator. Perches conspicuousl
on a bush or tree.

Food	Nest	Active Period
	2-3	
Habitat	**Sociability**	**Migratio**

Sombre Greenbul
(Sombre Bulbul)
Andropadus importunus **572**
Gewone Willie
Larger than a sparrow. This nondescrip
olive-green bird has characteristic whit
eyes. It favours dense riverine growt
where it is easily overlooked. A shy, ver
vocal bird that dives quickly into cove
when alarmed. The call is a penetratin
"willie" or "willie, come-and-have-a-figh
scaaaaared".

Food	Nest	Active Period
	1-3	
Habitat	**Sociability**	**Migratio**

Yellow-bellied Greenbul
(Yellow-bellied Bulbul)
Chlorocichla flaviventris **574**
Geelborswillie
Larger than a sparrow. It may be confuse
with the Sombre Greenbul but the yellow
underparts, dark red eyes (not white
and white eyelids are diagnostic. Th
upperparts are dull greenish. Forages a
all levels in riverine thickets, but prefer
the lower parts. A very vocal, but sh
bird.

Food	Nest	Active Period
	1-3	
Habitat	**Sociability**	**Migratio**

African Pipit (Grassveld Pipit)
Anthus cinnamomeus **716**
Gewone Koester

Larger than a sparrow. An indistinct terrestrial bird with an upright posture and long legs. The head and back are lightly streaked while the chest is more distinctly spotted. The belly is creamy-white and the base of the bill is yellow. Common in the Park and usually found in open areas with short grass. Runs in small bursts.

Food	Nest	Active Period
	2-4	

Habitat	Sociability	Migration
		◯

Burger Cillié

Yellow-throated Longclaw
Macronyx croceus **728**
Geelkeelkalkoentjie

Larger than a sparrow. The only bird in the Park that has a bright yellow throat bordered by a black band. The upperparts are brownish while the underparts and eyebrow are bright yellow. When disturbed, it may crouch on the ground or fly to a perch. It forages and roosts on the ground; prefers tall grass where it walks with long strides.

Food	Nest	Active Period
	2-4	

Habitat	Sociability	Migration
		◯

Burger Cillié

African Pied Wagtail
Motacilla aguimp **711**
Afrikaanse Bontkwikkie

Larger than a sparrow. This large wagtail has a contrasting black-and-white plumage. The upperparts, tail and chest are black in adult birds, and brownish in immatures. Seen on the lawns of rest camps and in the vicinity of rivers and dams. It regularly baths in shallow water. Non-breeding birds roost communally. A tame bird.

Food	Nest	Active Period
	3-5	

Habitat	Sociability	Migration
		◯

Burger Cillié

Insectivores with Medium-sized Bills

Monotonous Lark
Mirafra passerina 493
Bosveldlewerik

Sparrow-sized. A nondescript lark that resembles a female bishop. The white throat is conspicuous when singing. Occurs in grassland or open bushveld. Easily overlooked, except during the breeding season when the males sing: a monotonously repeated (by day or night) "for syrup is sweet" or "willow way wit". Has a short display flight.

Food	Nest	Active Period
	2-4	

Habitat	Sociability	Migration

Rufous-naped Lark
Mirafra africana 494
Rooineklewerik

A fairly large yellow-brown lark; larger than a sparrow. The rufous nape is seldom visible in the field. The rufous colouring in the wings may be seen in flight. During summer the male perches conspicuously from where it delivers its loud "tiree-tireoo" song. It prefers open grassveld with sparse trees or shrubs. Widespread and common.

Food	Nest	Active Period
	2-4	

Habitat	Sociability	Migration

Sabota Lark
Calendulauda sabota 498
Sabotalewerik

Larger than a sparrow. This streaked lark has a prominent white eyebrow that runs from the base of the bill to the nape. The pattern on the cheeks is characteristic. It is a common savanna species and widespread in the Park. It forages on the ground, but calls from a perch. The call is melodious, but variable and includes imitations of other birds.

Food	Nest	Active Period
	2-4	

Habitat	Sociability	Migration

Spotted Flycatcher
Muscicapa striata **689**
Europese Vlieëvanger

Larger than a sparrow. The streaked forehead and chest of this brownish flycatcher distinguish it from other flycatchers. It will dart after insects in flight and then return to its fairly low perch. It is quiet and flicks its wings more often than other flycatchers. A common summer migrant that is found throughout the Park.

Food	Nest	Active Period
	EURASIA	

Habitat	Sociability	Migration

Niel Cillié

African Paradise-Flycatcher
Terpsiphone viridis **710**
Paradysvlieëvanger

Larger than a sparrow. The dark blue head and chest, blue bill and eye-rings, chestnut back and tail are diagnostic. The male's long tail is almost twice the length of its body. The female has a shorter tail and duller eye-rings. Despite this bird's bright colouring it is easily overlooked, as it prefers dense vegetation with tall trees.

Food	Nest	Active Period
	2-4	

Habitat	Sociability	Migration

Burger Cillié (2)

Red-billed Oxpecker
Buphagus erythrorhynchus **772**
Rooibekrenostervoël

Smaller than a dove. The all-red bill and yellow eye-wattles of this oxpecker are diagnostic. (The scarcer Yellow-billed Oxpecker has a red bill with a yellow tip and a pale rump, but lacks the yellow eye-wattle.) Their habit of clinging to game in search of parasites makes oxpeckers unmistakable. If disturbed, it will move to the far side of the host or fly off.

Food	Nest	Active Period
	 2-5	

Habitat	Sociability	Migration

Burger Cillié

Insectivores with Medium-sized Bills

Burger Cillié

Ulrich Oberprieler

Wattled Starling
Creatophora cinerea 760
Lelspreeu
Smaller than a dove. This pale starling has black-tipped wings and a white rump (visible in flight). The breeding male has an unmistakable yellow-and black head with black wattles on the head and throat. The non-breeding male resembles the grey female. It roosts and nests communally in big untidy nests. common but nomadic bird.

Food	Nest	Active Period
	2-5	

Habitat	Sociability	Migratio

Burchell's Starling
Lamprotornis australis 762
Grootglansspreeu
About dove-sized. This starling differ from Meve's Starling in that it is large and more heavily built with a slight shorter, rounded tail. It has dark eye It is a common breeding resident sou of the Olifants river, less common the north. It forages on the ground an scavenges at picnic sites. Birds roo communally.

Lizeth Cillié

Food	Nest	Active Perio
	2-4	

Habitat	Sociability	Migratic

Meve's Starling
(Meve's Long-tailed Starling)
Lamprotornis mevesii 763
Langstertglansspreeu
About dove-sized. May be distinguishe from the similar Burchell's Starling by i extremely long and pointed tail. It ha dark eyes. Forages on the ground an prefers open areas with tall trees. Is on present in the Limpopo/Livuvhu riv system, where Burchell's Starling doe not occur.

Burger Cillié

Food	Nest	Active Perio
	3-4	

Habitat	Sociability	Migratic

96

Violet-backed Starling
(Plum-coloured Starling)
Cinnyricinclus leucogaster 761
Witborsspreeu

A small starling: smaller than a dove. The male is unmistakable with distinct glossy purple upperparts and throat and contrasting white underparts. The female is brown with heavily streaked underparts, but is distinguished by her yellow gape and eyes. Flocks are often seen feeding in fruiting trees.

Food	Nest	Active Period
	 2-4	

Habitat	Sociability	Migration

Cape Glossy Starling
(Glossy Starling)
Lamprotornis nitens 764
Kleinglansspreeu

Smaller than a dove. The eyes are orange. May be distinguished from the Greater Blue-eared Starling by its entirely metallic blue-green colour (including the flanks and belly), also lacking a facial mask. Less common than the Greater Blue-eared Starling and also not as tame. Less often seen in rest camps.

Food	Nest	Active Period
	 2-6	

Habitat	Sociability	Migration

Greater Blue-eared Starling
Lamprotornis chalybaeus 765
Grootblouoorglansspreeu

Smaller than a dove. The eyes are orange. It differs from the Cape Glossy Starling in that it has dark ear-coverts and a royal blue belly and flanks. It also has two rows of dark spots on the upper wing. It forages on the ground or in trees and is often seen in rest camps and picnic sites where it becomes very confiding.

Food	Nest	Active Period
	 2-5	

Habitat	Sociability	Migration

Small Insectivores with Tiny Bills

All the birds in this group are very small. For this reason their small bills may appear to be pointed where in fact they do have the slightly decurved upper jaw of the typical insectivores.

The white-eyes are a group of yellow-greenish birds with a characteristic white eye-ring of small feathers. They not only feed on insects, but also on soft fruit and nectar. The Cape White-eye is widespread in the Park, while the Yellow White-eye is confined to the far north.

Most birds in this group are warbler-like. As they are difficult to observe and identify only a small selection have been included in this guide. The scientific name has often been included in the common name, hence strange-sounding words such as prinia, cisticola, camaroptera and apalis.

These birds usually forage within the shelter of vegetation and are thus not easily seen. Some species have characteristic calls which facilitate their identification.

Cape White-eye
Zosterops virens 796
Kaapse Glasogie
A very small greenish-yellow bird with a conspicuous white eye-ring (absent in the immature bird). The crown and upperparts are olive-green, the under parts are yellow-green. (The yellow White-eye is more yellow all over, It is restricted to the Limpopo/Levuvhu river system.) Forages in small groups, and usually occurs along the larger rivers.

Food	Nest	Active Period
	1-4	

Habitat	Sociability	Migration

Long-billed Crombec
Sylvietta rufescens 651
Bosveldstompstert
A very small bird that appears tailless due to the extremely short tail. The upperparts are grey-brown and the underparts are cinnamon. It has a creamy-white eyebrow, a dark line through the eyes and a long bill. Active and restless, it forages in trees and bushes, working its way up from the lower levels.

Food	Nest	Active Period
	1-3	

Habitat	Sociability	Migration

Green-backed Camaroptera
(Green-backed Bleating Warbler)
Camaroptera brachyura **657**
Groenrugkwêkwêvoël

A very small bird. The olive-green back distinguishes it from the Grey-backed Camaroptera which has a grey back and is limited to the far north. The tail is usually raised. It forages in thickets. Secretive but noisy, it can be located by its call: a loud and snapping "k-wit". The alarm call sounds like a bleating lamb.

Food	Nest	Active Period
	2-4	

Habitat	Sociability	Migration

Grey-backed Camaroptera

Niel Cillié (2)

Tawny-flanked Prinia
Prinia subflava **683**
Bruinsylangstertjie

A very small bird with a long tail that is often held upright. The upperparts are grey-brown. The underparts are white and the flanks tawny. This usually tame bird is noisy and lively. It wags its raised tail sideways when alarmed. Pairs or small groups forage in grass or low down in shrubs and trees, often near water. Conspicuous.

Food	Nest	Active Period
	3-5	

Habitat	Sociability	Migration

Niel Cillié

Yellow-breasted Apalis
Apalis flivida **648**
Geelborskleinjantjie

A very small bird. The combination of a grey head, white throat and belly, red eyes and yellow chest are diagnostic. Males have a black bar below the yellow chest. It prefers thickets in a thornveld habitat where it forages restlessly by gleaning insects from twigs and leaves. Very vocal. It is a common resident in the Park.

Food	Nest	Active Period
	2-3	

Habitat	Sociability	Migration

♀

♂

Niel Cillié (2)

Small Insectivores with Tiny Bills

Burger Cillié

Chestnut-vented Tit-Babbler
Parisoma subcaeruleum 621
Bosveldtjeriktik

A small grey bird with a characteristic chestnut vent and white eyes. The throat and chest are boldly streaked black. Prefers dryer thornveld. It moves quickly through the middle and upper parts of trees and shrubs in search of food. Its "cherik-tiktik" call has given rise to the Afrikaans name. Also has a loud and melodious song.

Food	Nest	Active Period
	2-4	

Habitat	Sociability	Migration

Burger Cillié

Neddicky
Cisticola fulvicapilla 681
Neddikkie

A very small, brown bird. It is distinguished form other cisticolas by its fairly short tail, the uniform brown back and the rufous crown. It prefers the grassy understorey of woodland and savanna. The song is a soft, penetrating "weep weep weep". The "krrrrrr-r-r-r-r-r-r-r-r-r" alarm call sounds like running a fingernail across the teeth of a comb.

Food	Nest	Active Period
	2-4	

Habitat	Sociability	Migration

Niel Cillié

Rattling Cisticola
Cisticola chiniana 672
Bosveldtinktinkie

A very small bird. The most conspicuous cisticola in the Park where it occurs in a variety of savanna habitats. The tail is fairly long and the back is patterned. The male often perches on top of a tree or bush while singing its characteristic song of two to four introductory whistles followed by a trill or rattle. Utters a harsh alarm call.

Food	Nest	Active Period

	3-5	

Habitat	Sociability	Migration

Most seedeaters are finch-like or sparrow-like in appearance: they are small birds with stout conical bills. Most species forage on the ground, but others may cling to grass stems or branches while feeding.

In some species the male and female are alike, in others they are different. These differences may be permanent (e.g. the sparrows, waxbills, firefinches, pytilias, canaries, buntings and some weavers), or just during the breeding season. In most weavers as well as the bishops, widowbirds, queleas and whydahs the males are characteristically coloured during the breeding season, but resemble the dully coloured females in winter. Then they are most difficult to identify.

The sparrows have an overall brownish appearance. Male weavers build intricately woven nests. Most males are predominantly yellow during the breeding season. The waxbills are a group of very small, brightly coloured seedeaters. Those that are mainly red in colour are known as firefinches. The male whydahs are distinguished by their long tails during the breeding season. All whydahs are brood parasites which lay their eggs into the nest of a host species.

The doves and larger pigeons need no introduction. They swallow seeds whole, often feeding on larger seeds than the other seedeaters.

House Sparrow
Passer domesticus 801
Huismossie

The male has a grey crown and rump, a black throat and bill, and white cheeks. The much paler female has a pinkish-brown bill and an indistinct creamy eyebrow. An introduced species that is usually found around human habitation. It thus occurs in rest camps and at picnic sites and becomes fairly tame, but remains wary.

Food	Nest	Active Period
	3-6	

Habitat	Sociability	Migration

Southern Grey-headed Sparrow
Passer diffusus 804
Gryskopmossie

It may be distinguished from other sparrows by its all-grey head and the white wing-bar. The back is chestnut brown. Common throughout the Park, even in rest camps, where they some-times join House Sparrows to feed. Forages by hopping or walking on the ground. Breeds in suitable holes in trees or walls.

Food	Nest	Active Period
	3-5	

Habitat	Sociability	Migration

Seedeaters

Burger Cillié (2)

♂
♀

Village Weaver
(Spotted-backed Weaver)
Ploceus cucullatus 811
Bontrugwewer

About sparrow-sized. The breeding male is distinguished from the Southern Masked-Weaver by the yellow forehead and mottled back. The female and non-breeding male have whitish underparts and mottled olive-yellow upperparts. Usually found close to streams where they breed in reeds or trees.

Food	Nest	Active Period
	2-5	

Habitat	Sociability	Migration

Niel Cillié (2)

♂
♀

Southern Masked-Weaver
Ploceus velatus 814
Swartkeelgeelvink

About sparrow-sized. The breeding male differs from the male Village Weaver in the black mask that extends onto the forehead, and the relatively uniform yellowish upperparts. The female and non-breeding male have olive-yellow upperparts with streaks on the back and much paler underparts. The nest is neatly woven.

Food	Nest	Active Period
	2-4	

Habitat	Sociability	Migration

Burger Cillié (2)

♂
♀

Lesser Masked-Weaver
Ploceus intermedius 815
Kleingeelvink

About sparrow-sized. The breeding male differs from the other two black-faced weavers in that it has pale eyes and the mask extends onto the mid-crown. The female and non-breeding male are more yellow than the other weavers. It breeds in colonies, usually in reeds and large trees near water. The neatly woven nest has a short entrance tunnel.

Food	Nest	Active Period
	2-4	

Habitat	Sociability	Migration

Spectacled Weaver
Ploceus ocularis 810
Brilwewer
About sparrow-sized. This weaver has a sharply pointed, black bill, a diagnostic black line through the pale yellow eyes and a chestnut-brown wash over the head. The male has a black throat. It forages for insects amongst the foliage of trees and shrubs. A shy bird that is more often heard than seen. The woven nest has a long entrance tunnel.

Food	Nest	Active Period
	  2-3	

Habitat	Sociability	Migration

Red-headed Weaver
Anaplectes melanotis 819
Rooikopwewer
About sparrow-sized. The breeding male has a bright red head, chest and mantle; non-breeding males and females are yellowish. Both sexes have pinkish-orange bills and white bellies. A quiet weaver that is easily overlooked. The untidy nest is woven out of sticks and thin plant material. It has a long entrance tunnel.

Food	Nest	Active Period
	  2-3	

Habitat	Sociability	Migration

Red-billed Buffalo-Weaver
Bubalornis niger 798
Buffelwewer
Larger than a sparrow. The black plumage, robust red bill and white wing-patches distinguish this large noisy weaver. The female is browner, has a paler bill and the underparts are mottled with white. It prefers large trees like Baobabs and roosts communally in large, untidy twig nests. Forages on the ground.

Food	Nest	Active Period
	  2-4	

Habitat	Sociability	Migration

103

Seedeaters

Niel Cillié

Yellow-throated Petronia
(Yellow-throated Sparrow)
Petronia superciliaris 805
Geelvlekmossie

About sparrow-sized. This bird is best identified by the conspicuous creamy-white eyebrows, broadening behind the eyes. The yellow throat-spot is diagnostic but very difficult to see in the field. Fairly common and widespread throughout the Park. Prefers areas of tall broad-leaved woodland.

Food	Nest	Active Period
	1-5	

Habitat	Sociability	Migration

Ulrich Oberprieler

Blue Waxbill
Uraeginthus angolensis 844
Gewone Blousysie

Smaller than a sparrow. The face, throat, chest, flanks, tail and rump of the male are powder blue. The female is paler and the blue is confined to the face and chest. The upperparts are brown. It forages on the ground and becomes tame at rest camps. The flock flies into the nearest tree when disturbed. A well known and widespread bird.

Food	Nest	Active Period
	2-7	

Habitat	Sociability	Migration

Ulrich Oberprieler

Common Waxbill
Estrilda astrild 846
Rooibeksysie

A small waxbill with a red bill and diagnostic red eye-stripes. It appears brownish from a distance, but at close range the finely barred body with the central red belly-patch becomes visible. The immature has a black bill. It is normally seen in small flocks in grassy areas and reed-beds, often near water. Easily overlooked.

Food	Nest	Active Period
	3-9	

Habitat	Sociability	Migration

Southern Red Bishop
Euplectes orix 824
Suidelike Rooivink

Although not common in the Park, one cannot overlook the breeding male's red-and-black plumage. Females and non-breeding males are small brown birds with characteristic streaks on the chest. Red Bishops inhabit lush grass and reed beds. During the breeding season males display by puffing up their distinctive plumage.

Food	Nest	Active Period
	2-5	

Habitat	Sociability	Migration

Jameson's Firefinch
Lagonosticta rhodopareia 841
Jamesonse Vuurvinkie

A very small bird. Both sexes have white spots on the flanks and dark blue bills. It lacks the grey crown and nape of the African Firefinch and thus appears more red. The male is reddish-pink on the head and underparts, while the female is much paler. Prefers grass and shrubby areas in savannna and bushveld. Forages on the ground.

Food	Nest	Active Period
	2-5	

Habitat	Sociability	Migration

Red-billed Firefinch
Lagonosticta senegala 842
Rooibekvuurvinkie

A very small bird. Its pink (not blue) bill and yellow eye-ring distinguish both the male and female from other firefinches. The male is the reddest of all firefinches. The female is overall sandy brown, with only the rump and undertail pink. It prefers thickets with open patches of grass, where it forages on the ground. Easily overlooked.

Food	Nest	Active Period
	2-5	

Habitat	Sociability	Migration

Seedeaters

Red-billed Quelea
Quelea quelea 821
Rooibekkwelea
About sparrow-sized. The breeding male has a bright red bill and usually a black mask, edged with red or yellow. The breeding female has a yellow bill. Non-breeding birds are dull mouse-coloured (heavily streaked above) with creamy-white eyebrows and red bills. Often occurs in huge flocks. Breeds in large colonies in thorn trees.

Food	Nest	Active Period
	2-5	
Habitat	**Sociability**	**Migration**

Green-winged Pytilia
(Melba Finch)
Pytilia melba 834
Gewone Melba
Slightly smaller than a sparrow. The male has a red bill, forecrown and throat with a grey hindcrown and nape. The female has a red bill with an overall grey head. Both sexes have heavily barred underparts and yellowish-green upperparts. Prefers thickets with rank grass. It forages mostly on the ground.

Food	Nest	Active Period
	2-5	
Habitat	**Sociability**	**Migration**

Bronze Mannikin
Spermestes cucullatus 857
Gewone Fret
A very small bird. The black head, white underparts, brown upperparts and barred flanks are diagnostic. This bird has a bicoloured bill with the upper jaw black and the lower greyish. In good sunlight the bronze-green patch on the wings is visible. Immatures are brown. Forages in groups on the ground or on grass. Flicks its wings and tail when alarmed.

Food	Nest	Active Period
	2-8	
Habitat	**Sociability**	**Migration**

Yellow-fronted Canary
(Yellow-eyed Canary)
Crithagra mozambicus **869**
Geeloogkanarie

Smaller than a sparrow. The dark line through the eyes and the black moustachial stripe are diagnostic. The underparts are bright yellow, fading to a paler yellow on the flanks. Often occurs in the rest camps. Roosts in a small flock. Forages mainly on the ground. When disturbed it flies into nearest tree.

Food	Nest	Active Period
	 2-5	

Habitat	Sociability	Migration

Niel Cillié

Golden-breasted Bunting
Emberiza flaviventris **884**
Rooirugstreepkoppie

About sparrow-sized. A very attractive bird. The black and white stripes on the head, the golden-yellow underparts and chestnut mantle are diagnostic. The female is duller than the male. When flushed, it flies into a tree, displaying its white outer tail-feathers. It forages mainly in the open, but sings from a perch in a tree.

Food	Nest	Active Period
	 2-4	

Habitat	Sociability	Migration

Peter Barachievy

Cinnamon-breasted Bunting
(Cinnamon-breasted Rock Bunting)
Emberiza tahapisi **886**
Klipstreepkoppie

About sparrow-sized. The male's cinnamon underparts and boldly striped head are characteristic. The female and immature are duller, the head pattern less bold. It forages on the ground and prefers rocky outcrops or stony areas. When disturbed it flies off to perch on a rock.

Food	Nest	Active Period
	 2-4	

Habitat	Sociability	Migration

Burger Cillié (2)

♂

♀

107

Seedeaters

Pin-tailed Whydah
♂

Vidua macroura **860**

Koningrooibekkie

About sparrow-sized. The breeding male has a red bill, a white collar and underparts, as well as a very long tail. The female and non-breeding male have a tawny plumage, red bill, grey legs and boldly striped heads. The breeding male is very aggressive towards other birds. A brood parasite of mainly the Common Waxbill.

Food	Nest	Active Period
	BREEDING PARASITE	
Habitat	Sociability	Migration

Long-tailed Paradise-Whydah
♂
(Eastern Paradise Whydah)

Vidua paradisaea **862**

Gewone Paradysvink

About sparrow-sized. The breeding male is easily identified by its bold colour pattern and the characteristically shaped long tail. The female and non-breeding male are brownish with dark stripes on the head. Conspicuous. It forages on the ground. A brood parasite of the Green-winged Pytilia.

Food	Nest	Active Period
	BREEDING PARASITE	
Habitat	Sociability	Migration

White-winged Widowbird
♂
(White-winged Widow)

Euplectes albonotatus **829**

Witvlerkflap

About sparrow-sized. The breeding male is black with yellow shoulders, white wing-patches and a blue-grey bill. The male fans his tail during display. The brown non-breeding male may be distinguished from the female by the coloured wing-patches. Prefers moist patches in grassland and thornveld.

Food	Nest	Active Period
	2-5	
Habitat	Sociability	Migration

Red-eyed Dove
Streptopelia semitorquata 352
Grootringduif

The largest of the half-collared doves. The underparts are slightly pinkish. At close range the red eye and bare patch around the eye may be seen. The tail lacks any white feathers. A wary bird that forages on the ground. It prefers areas with large trees where it roosts and breeds. The call is a characteristic "I-am...a-Red-eyed-Dove".

Food	Nest	Active Period
	2	

Habitat	Sociability	Migration

Niel Cillié

African Mourning Dove
Streptopelia decipiens 353
Rooioogtortelduif

This dove may be confused with the Cape Turtle Dove, but is distinguished by the red skin around the pale yellow eyes and the pinkish underparts. The tips of the outer tail-feathers are white. Forages on the ground. Most common in some of the central rest camps where they are very tame. The call is a soft "krrrow-rrrrrrrrrrrrr".

Food	Nest	Active Period
	2	

Habitat	Sociability	Migration

Niel Cillié

Cape Turtle-Dove
Streptopelia capicola 354
Gewone Tortelduif

It may be distinguished from the African Mourning Dove and Red-eyed Dove by its pale grey plumage and dark eyes without any bare skin around them. The outer tail-feathers are white. Forages on the ground and roosts in trees. Groups may be seen at waterholes in the early morning and late afternoon. The call is well known "work harrr-der".

Food	Nest	Active Period
	2	

Habitat	Sociability	Migration

Niel Cillié

Seedeaters

Laughing Dove
Streptopelia senegalensis 355
Rooiborsduifie
It differs from the other greyish doves in that it lacks the ring on the hindneck. The chest is rufous with black speckles. The white outer tail-feathers are visible in flight. Common throughout the Park. Drinks water regularly and forages on the ground. The call reminds one of somebody laughing. Becomes very tame and confiding.

Food	Nest	Active Period
	 2	

Habitat	Sociability	Migration

Namaqua Dove
Oena capensis 356
Namakwaduifie
This small dove is unmistakable with its long tail, bands across the back and chestnut flight-feathers. The male has a black face and throat, as well as an orange-yellow bill with a purple base, both of which are lacking in the female. The immature is heavily spotted. Occurs erratically in the Park, preferring areas with very short grass.

Food	Nest	Active Period
	 2	

Habitat	Sociability	Migration

Emerald-spotted Wood-Dove
(Green-spotted Dove)
Turtur chalcospilos 358
Groenvlekduifie
A small dove with characteristic green iridescent spots on the wings. It has a bluish-grey head. The bands across the rump and the rufous wingtips are visible in flight. Forages on the ground and drinks water frequently. It takes off very quickly. The call is a melancholic "du du du du".

Food	Nest	Active Period
	 2	

Habitat	Sociability	Migration

REPTILES AND AMPHIBIANS

These are cold-blooded vertebrates. Reptiles have a scaly skin, while that of amphibians is naked. Although a large variety of species occur in the Park, they are rarely seen due to their smaller size and nocturnal lifestyles.

Reptiles

Snakes, lizards, monitors, agamas, chameleons, crocodiles, tortoises and terrapins

Amphibians

Frogs and toads

Reptiles

The well-known Nile Crocodile is the Park's largest reptile. It occurs in all permanent water bodies and may even move to small temporary pans.

In addition to the Leopard Tortoise described in this guide, the Natal and Speke's Hinged Tortoises also occur in the Park. The Serrated Hinged Terrapin is a very conspicuous species, while the Pan Hinged Terrapin is confined to the far north. The Marsh Terrapin is the smaller, flat terrapin seen in the Park.

Over 55 lizard species have been recorded in the Park. As most of them are small, shy and difficult to identify, only a handful are described here.

In spite of the fact that most people are fascinated by snakes, they are rarely seen in the Park. The Southern African Python is the largest and the Black Mamba the most venomous snake found here. Other highly venomous snakes are the Mozambique Spitting Cobra, Snouted Cobra, Puff Adder and Boomslang. The other 50-odd snakes found in the Park are either completely harmless to people or their venom does not pose any serious threat. Always remember that snakes are not aggressive, but they may bite in self-defence!

Burger Cillié

Spotted Bush-Snake
Philothamnus semivariegatus
Gespikkelde Bosslang
This harmless snake is often mistaken for the Green Mamba (which does not occur in the Park) or the Boomslang. It is characterised by the dark markings on the front part of its green body. This diurnal, active snake lives mainly in trees where it hunts geckos, lizards, frogs and chameleons. It inflates its neck when threatened.

Length	Active Period
80 - 100 cm	☼

Habitat	Food

Ulrich Oberprieler

Puff Adder
Bitis arietans arietans
Pofadder
The largest adder in the Park. It has a thick body and triangular head. The brown body is marked with dark creamy-edged chevrons. It is a slow and inactive snake which relies on its camouflaging colour to catch its prey. It inflates in defence and releases the air with a loud puffing sound, hence the name. Highly venomous.

Length	Active Period
60 - 100 cm	☼ ☾

Habitat	Food

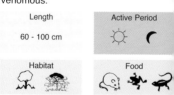

Snouted Cobra
Naja annulifera
Bosveldkobra / Wipneuskobra

This large cobra is yellowish to grey-brown above and yellowish below. Some individuals have broad, pale bands across their bodies. It is widespread in the lowveld, but is not often seen, as it is active mainly at night. Although being able to spread an impressive hood and being highly venomous, the Snouted Cobra is not an aggressive snake.

Length	Active Period
120 - 250 cm	

Habitat	Food

Ulrich Oberprieler

Mozambique Spitting Cobra
Naja mossambica
Mosambiekse Spoegkobra

A smallish, grey-brown to dark olive cobra, averaging 1,2m in length. The underparts are slightly pinkish with dark bands across the throat. When threatened it "spits" its potent venom readily, with or without raising a hood. This cobra is common in the Park, preferring rocky country or other shelter where it hides during the day.

Length	Active Period
100 - 150 cm	

Habitat	Food

Warren Schmidt

Black Mamba
Dendroaspis polylepis
Swartmamba

In spite of its name, this highly venomous snake is rarely black, but rather a grey to dark olive-brown colour. It is a long and slender, often over 3m in length. The head is coffin-shaped with a long, "smiling" mouth. It is shy, but very aggressive and dangerous when threatened. It rears a large part of its fore body and may bite repeatedly.

Length	Active Period
250 - 350 cm	

Habitat	Food

Warren Schmidt

113

Reptiles

Lizeth Cillié

Southern African Python
Python natalensis
Suider-Afrikaanse Luislang
The largest snake in the Park, up to abou 5m in length. The olive-coloured skin is decorated by beautiful dark patterns and patches. It is non-venomous, but bites its prey, then curling around it to suffocate it. Prey is swallowed whole and head first. It is fond of water, but may be seen basking in the sun.

Length	Active Period
300 - 550 cm	

Habitat	Food

Burger Cillié

Rock Monitor
Varanus albigularis
Veldlikkewaan
Unlike the larger Water Monitor, this monitor (leguaan) is usually found away from water. It has a shorter tail than the Water Monitor and holds its head in line with the body, not above. The dark stripe from the eye to the shoulder is diagnostic. It hides in tree holes or amongst rocks, but actively hunts a variety of smaller prey.

Length	Active Period
70 - 130 cm	☼

Habitat	Food

Lizeth Cillié

Water Monitor
Varanus niloticus
Waterlikkewaan
This large monitor (leguaan) is usually seen near water where it hunts frogs, crabs, small fish, insects and even small mammals and birds. It swims readily using its long flattened tail for propulsion while pressing its legs against its body. On land it holds its head well above the ground. It is fond of sunbathing at the water's edge.

Length	Active Period
100 - 180 cm	☼

Habitat	Food

Rainbow Rock Skink
Mabuya quinquetaeniata margaritifer
Bloustert-koppieskink

A large, beautifully coloured lizard. Juveniles and females are dark olive-brown to black, with three white bands extending from head to tail, where they widen and change into bright blue. Males are olive brown with yellow or orange tails. Confined to rocky outcrops where they are often seen while hunting insects.

Length	Active Period
20 - 27 cm	☼

Habitat	Food

Niel Cillié (2)

Giant Plated Lizard
Gerrhosaurus validus validus
Reuse-pantserakkedis

A large lizard with characteristic large, heavy scales. It is dark brown in colour with yellow spots on the back and irregular creamy-white bands on the sides. It is typical of the rocky outcrops in the Park, but remains shy and wary. Giant Plated Lizards feed on both invertebrates and soft plant material such as leaves and fruit.

Length	Active Period
40 - 60 cm	☼

Habitat	Food

Burger Cillié

Striped Skink
Trachylepis punctatissima
Gestreepte Akkedis

This well-known lizard is widespread in the Lowveld. It is olive to dark brown above with a characteristic creamy stripe along either side of the back. The underparts are creamy-white. It forages on rocks and trees and is very fond of sun-bathing. Like many skinks, the female does not lay eggs, but gives birth to live young.

Length	Active Period
18 - 21 cm	☼

Habitat	Food

Niel Cillié

Reptiles

Nile Crocodile
Crocodylus niloticus
Nylkrokodil

This unmistakable, water-living reptile occurs throughout the Park. Baby crocodiles feed mostly on insects and other invertebrates, while adult take a variety of larger prey, from fish to antelope. As their teeth are adapted for grasping and not chewing, crocodiles tear bits of flesh from a carcass by spinning their bodies.

Length	Active Period
250 - 350 cm	

Habitat	Food

Southern Tree Agama
Acanthocerus atricollis atricollis
Boomkoggelmander

These large agamas are often seen on the trunks of trees. The broad head is a brilliant blue, larger and brighter in males than females. When disturbed they retreat around the tree truck to the opposite side. Males bob their heads up and down when displaying. In spite of their ferocious appearance, they are not venomous.

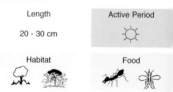

Length	Active Period
20 - 30 cm	

Habitat	Food

Moreau's Tropical House Gecko
Hemidactylus mabouia
Tropiese Huisgeitjie

A medium-sized gecko with a flattened body and large eyes with vertical pupils. The grey-brown back has dark spots. Often found under tree bark, but also enters houses at night in search of insects and other suitable prey. The males are highly territorial. Intruders are attacked immediately and vicious fights may result.

Length	Active Period
12 - 16 cm	

Habitat	Food

Flap-necked Chameleon
Chamaeleo dilepis
Gewone Verkleurmannetjie
The only chameleon to occur in the Park. Like other chameleons, it changes its colour to blend in with the background. It inflates its body and hisses loudly when threatened. In spite of this impressive display, it is not venomous. It catches insects by extending its long sticky tongue. The eyes move independently from each other.

Length	Active Period
20 - 25 cm	☀

Habitat	Food

Ulrich Oberprieler

Leopard Tortoise
Geochelone pardalis
Bergskilpad
This large, well-known tortoise is widespread in Southern Africa. It may be distinguished from the hinged tortoises by its domed shell, lacking the hinge at the back. The colour of the shell varies from yellow with black spots in young animals to dark brown, heavily streaked and blotched in older animals. Occurs throughout the Park.

Length	Active Period
30 - 45 cm	☀

Habitat	Food

Lizeth Cillié

Serrated Hinged Terrapin
Pelusios sinuatis
Skarnierdopwaterskilpad
The well-domed, rounded shell distinguishes this large terrapin from the smaller, flattened Marsh Terrapin. They prefer permanent rivers and waterholes and are fond of sunbathing on a rock or log. They feed on a variety of prey (such as frogs, insects, crabs and mussels) and regularly scavenge on carcasses in the water.

Length	Active Period
30 - 40 cm	☀

Habitat	Food

Burger Cillié

117

Amphibians

The roughly 35 frog species of the Park vary in size from the African Bullfrog (maximum 115mm) to the tiny Dwarf Puddle Frog which does not grow bigger than 19mm. Most of them are widely distributed in the Lowveld, but a few are confined to the higher-lying south-western regions. In addition, a very small number of specialised frogs occur in a few isolated habitats.

Frogs are not often seen by visitors. This is not only because they are small and tend to hide in water or under vegetation, but also because most frogs are nocturnal creatures. The easiest way to find them is to search the rest camps at night. Smaller ponds and even the moist ablution blocks attract quite a number of species.

Frogs usually hibernate during the dry winter month. They may bury underground or in other suitable shelter until the first summer rains. Then they emerge in their hundreds: it seems to "have rained frogs"! The males become very vociferous in their effort to attract a mate. (As each frog species has a unique call, this is a good way to identify the various species.) Soon the eggs are laid and the tadpoles hatched. A huge number of animals prey on the tadpoles, but a few reach adulthood and the species survives.

Niel Cillié

African Bullfrog
Pyxicephalus edulis
Kleinbrulpadda
These bullfrogs have large, square and thick-set bodies. The colour is dull green and mottled brown with whitish ridges on the back. The belly is smooth, creamy yellow in colour. Not often seen as it remains buried in sandy soil for most of the year. It breeds once the pans have filled after the summer rains. Then they may be seen during the day.

Length	Active Period
9 - 11 cm	

Habitat	Food

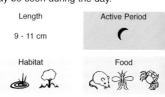

Niel Cillié

Foam Nest Frog
Chiromantis xerampelina
Skuimnespadda
These medium-sized tree frogs are usually grey or pale brown, but may change from very dark to almost white depending on the background. In summer their white foam nests are a common sight on branches above waterholes. The eggs develop within two to four days into tadpoles which drop into the water after another two days,

Length	Active Period
5 - 9 cm	

Habitat	Food

Guttural Toad
Bufo gutturalis
Gewone Skurwepadda
This large toad has a pair of dark patches on the snout and another pair behind the eyes. These demarcate a pale, cross-shaped area on the head. Males have dark throats. A very adap-table species occurring in higher-lying areas, where they breed in permanent waterholes. During the day they hide under logs, stones or other shelter.

Length	Active Period
10 cm	(

Habitat	Food
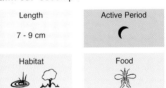	

Niel Cillié

Red Toad
Schismaderma carens
Rooirugskurwepadda
This large toad is pale brick-red above with two dark spots in the middle of the back and a greyish white belly. It occurs throughout the Park, but is not often seen during the day. Red Toads are "explosive breeders" and gather in huge numbers after good rains to breed in a favoured deep pool. The call is a loud, drawn-out "oooomp".

Length	Active Period
7 - 9 cm	(

Habitat	Food

Burger Cillié

Olive Toad
Bufo garmani
Noordelike Gevlekte Skurwepadda
This large, brightly coloured toad is widespread in the Park. Like most toads it is not often seen due to its nocturnal habits. It varies from dark brown to yellow-brown in colour, with brick-red or brown patches on then back. They frequently occur in the rest camps where their loud "aaawng" calls are heard during the summer breeding season.

Length	Active Period
10 cm	(

Habitat	Food

Transvaal Museum

119

Andrew Deacon

Plain Grass Frog
Ptychadena anchietae
Rooiruggraspadda

These frogs have angular bodies with pointed noses. They are red above with a pale triangle on the snout. The legs are paler than the back. The underparts are white and the lower belly is pale yellow. They prefer shallow marshes and pans in savanna and grassland. The call is a high-pitched trill, commonly heard in spring and summer.

Length	Active Period
4 - 5.5 cm	

Habitat	Food

Niel Cillié

Common River Frog
Afrana angolensis
Gewone Rivierpadda

A medium-sized, green-and-brown frog with dark spots. A yellow line usually runs from nose to tail. The large eyes bulge characteristically beyond the outline of the face when seen from above. The belly is smooth and white. It prefers streams in grasslands. When disturbed, these frogs take enormous leaps into the water.

Length	Active Period
4 - 8 cm	

Habitat	Food

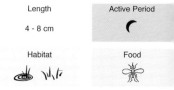

Andrew Deacon

Painted Reed Frog
Hyperolius marmoratus taeniatus
Gestreepte Rietpadda

A small frog, usually beautifully coloured with characteristic stripes along its body, but it may also occur in a golden-brown or lemon-yellow variety. When swimming, the red inner limbs and toe webbing are clearly visible. Prefer vegetation near pans and rest in the canopy of trees during the day. At night their loud, piercing whistles may be heard.

Length	Active Period
2.5 - 3.5 cm	

Habitat	Food

Mammal Checklist
The following mammals have been recorded in the Park

rdvark — Erdvark ☐
rdwolf — Aardwolf ☐
boon
  Chacma — Kaapse Bobbejaan ☑
dger
  Honey — Ratel ☐
.t
African Pipistrelle — Afrika-vlermuis ☐
African Yellow — Geel-dakvlermuis ☐
Anchieta's Pipistrelle — Anchieta-vlermuis ☐
Angola Free-tailed — Angola-losstertvlermuis ☐
Ansorge's Free-tailed — Ansorge-losstertvlermuis ☐
Banana — Piesangvlermuis ☐
Botswana Long-eared — Botswana-langoorvlermuis ☐
Bushveld Horseshoe — Bosveld-saalneusvlermuis ☐
Butterfly — Vlindervlermuis ☐
Cape Serotine — Kaapse Dakvlermuis ☐
Commerson's Roundleaf — Commerson-bladneusvlermuis ☐
Common Slit-faced — Gewone Spleetneusvlermuis ☐
Damara Woolly — Damara-wolhaarvlermuis ☐
Darling's Horseshoe — Darling-saalneusvlermuis ☐
Egyptian Free-tailed — Egiptiese Losstertvlermuis ☐
Egyptian Rousette — Egiptiese Vrugtevlermuis ☐
Geoffroy's Horseshoe — Geoffroy-saalneusvlermuis ☐
Hildebrandt's Horseshoe — Hildebrandt-saalneusvlermuis ☐
Lander's Horseshoe — Lander-saalneusvlermuis ☐
Lesser Woolly — Klein-wolhaarvlermuis ☐
Lesser Yellow House — Klein-geeldakvlermuis ☐
Little Free-tailed — Klein-losstertvlermuis ☐
Long-tailed Serotine — Langstert-dakvlermuis ☐
Madagascar Large Free-tailed — Madagaskar-grootlosstertvlermuis ☐
Melck's Serotine — Melck-dakvlermuis ☐
Midas Free-tailed — Midas-losstertvlermuis ☐
Peak-saddle Horseshoe — Spitssaalneus-vlermuis ☐
Peters' Epauletted Fruit — Peters-witkolvrugtevlermuis ☑
Rufus Hairy — Rooilanghaarvlermuis ☐
Rüppell's Horseshoe — Rüppell-saalneusvlermuis ☐
Rüppell's Pipistrelle — Rüppell-vlermuis ☐
Rusty — Roeskleurvlermuis ☐
Schlieffen's — Schlieffen-vlermuis ☐
Schreibers' Long-fingered — Schreibers-grotvlermuis ☐
Somali Serotine — Somali-dakvlermuis ☐
Sundevall's Roundleaf — Sundevall-bladneusvlermuis ☐
Swinny's Horseshoe — Swinny-saalneusvlermuis ☐

Temminck's Hairy — Temminck-langhaarvlermuis ☐
Tomb — Witlyfvlermuis ☐
Wahlberg's Epauletted Fruit — Wahlberg-witkolvrugtevlermuis ☐
Welwitsch's Hairy — Welwitsch-langhaarvlermuis ☐
Wood's Slit-faced — Wood-spleetneusvlermuis ☐
Buffalo
  African — Afrika-buffel ☑
Bushbuck — Bosbok ☐
Bushpig — Bosvark ☐
Canerat
  Greater — Grootrietrot ☐
Caracal — Rooikat ☐
Cat
  African Wild — Vaalboskat ☑
Cheetah — Jagluiperd ☐
Civet
  African — Afrika-siwet ☐
Dog
  African Wild — Wildehond ☑
Dormouse
  Woodland — Boswaaierstertmuis ☐
Duiker
  Common — Gewone Duiker ☐
  Red — Rooiduiker ☐
Eland — Eland ☐
Elephant
  African Savanna — Afrika-olifant ☑
Elephant-shrew
  Four-toed — Bosklaasneus ☐
  Eastern Rock — Oostelike Klipklaasneus ☐
  Short-shouted — Kortneusklaasneus ☐
Fox
  Bat-eared — Bakoorvos ☑
Galago (Bushbaby)
  South African — Suid-Afrikaanse Nagapie ☐
  Greater — Bosnagaap ☐
Genet
  Common
  Large-spotted — Rooikolmuskejaatkat ☐
  Small-spotted — Kleinkolmuskejaatkat ☐
Gerbil
  Bushveld — Bosveld-nagmuis ☑
Giraffe — Kameelperd ☑
Grysbok
  Sharpe's — Tropiese Grysbok ☐
Hare
  Cape — Vlakhaas ☐
  Scrub — Kolhaas ☐

continued on p122

Mammal Checklist

English	Afrikaans
Hartebeest	
Lichtenstein's	Mofhartbees
Hedgehog	
Southern African	SA Krimpvarkie
Hippopotamus	Seekoei
Hyaena	
Brown	Bruinhiëna
Spotted	Gevlekte Hiëna
Hyrax (Dassie)	
Rock	Klipdassie
Yellow-spotted Rock	Geelkoldassie
Impala	Rooibok
Jackal	
Black-backed	Rooijakkals
Side-striped	Witkwasjakkals
Klipspringer	Klipspringer
Kudu	Koedoe
Leopard	Luiperd
Lion	Leeu
Mole	
Juliana's Golden	Juliana se Gouemol
Yellow Golden	Geel-gouemol
Molerat	
African	Vaalmol
Mongoose	
Banded	Gebande Muishond
Dwarf	Dwergmuishond
Large Grey	Grootgrysmuishond
Marsh	Watermuishond
Meller's	Meller-muishond
Selous'	Kleinwitstertmuishond
Slender	Swartkwasmuishond
White-tailed	Witstertmuishond
Monkey	
Sykes' (Samango)	Samango-aap
Vervet	Blouaap
Mouse	
Chestnut Climbing	Roeskleurklimmuis
Fat	Vetmuis
Grey Climbing	Grysklimmuis
House	Huismuis
Southern	
Multimammate	Vaalveldmuis
Namaqua Rock	Namakwaland-klipmuis
Natal Multimammate	Natalse Vaalveldmuis
Pouched	Wangsakmuis
Pygmy	Dwergmuis
Spiny	Stekelmuis
Woodland	Woudmuis

English	Afrikaans	✓
Nyala	Njala	☐
Oribi	Oorbietjie	☐
Pangolin	Ietermagog	☐
Polecat		☐
Striped	Stinkmuishond	☑
Porcupine		
Cape	Suider-Afrikaanse Ystervark	☐
Rabbit		☑
Natal Red Rock	Natalse Rooiklipkonyn	☐
Rat		☐
Acacia	Boomrot	☐
Angoni Vlei	Angoni-vleirot	☑
Giant	Reuserot	☐
House	Huisrot	☐
Red Veld	Afrika-bosrot	☐
Water	Waterrot	☐
Reedbuck		☑
Mountain	Rooiribbok	☐
Southern	Rietbok	☐
Rhebok	Vaalribbok	☐
Rhinoceros		
Black	Swartrenoster	☐
White	Witrenoster	☑
Roan Antelope	Bastergemsbok	☐
Sable Antelope	Swartwitpens	☐
Serval	Tierboskat	☐
Shrew		☑
Greater Dwarf	Groter Dwergskeerbek	☐
Lesser Red Musk	Kleiner Rooiskeerbek	☐
Lesser Grey-brown		
Musk	Peters-skeerbek	☐
Reddish-Grey Musk	Rooigrysskeerbek	☐
Swamp Musk	Vleiskeerbek	☐
Tiny Musk	Dwergskeerbek	☐
Springhare	Springhaas	☐
Squirrel		☑
Tree	Boomeekhoring	☑
Steenbok	Steenbok	☑
Suni	Soenie	☐
Tsessebe	Basterhartbees	☐
Warthog		
Common	Vlakvark	☑
Waterbuck	Waterbok	☐
Wildebeest		
Blue	Blouwildebees	☑
Zebra		
Plains (Burchell's)	Vlaktekwagga (Bontsebra)	☑

Bird Checklist

The following birds have been recorded in the Park

No.	English	Afrikaans	
	Apalis		
45	Bar-throated	Bandkeelkleinjantjie	☐
48	Yellow-breasted	Geelborskleinjantjie	☐
	Avocet		
94	Pied	Bontelsie	☐
	Babbler		
60	Arrow-marked	Pylvlekkatlagter	☐
63	Southern Pied	Witkatlagter	☐
	Barbet		
65	Acacia Pied	Bonthoutkapper	☐
64	Black-collared	Rooikophoutkapper	☐
73	Crested	Kuifkophoutkapper	☐
46	Bateleur	Berghaan	☐
	Batis		
01	Chinspot	Witliesbosbontrokkie	☐
	Bee-eater		
40	Blue-cheeked	Blouwangbyvreter	☐
38	European	Europese Byvreter	☐
44	Little	Kleinbyvreter	☐
41	Southern Carmine	Rooiborsbyvreter	☐
45	Swallow-tailed	Swaelstertbyvreter	☐
43	White-fronted	Rooikeelbyvreter	☐
	Bishop		
24	Southern Red	Rooivink	☐
26	Yellow-crowned	Goudgeelvink	☐
	Bittern		
9	Dwarf	Dwergrietreier	☐
0	Eurasian	Grootrietreier	☐
3	Little	Kleinrietreier	☐
	Boubou		
36	Southern	Suidelike Waterfiskaal	☐
37	Tropical	Tropiese Waterfiskaal	☐
	Brownbul		
59	Terrestrial	Boskrapper	☐
41	Brubru	Bontroklaksman	☐
	Bulbul		
58	Dark-capped	Swartoogtiptol	☐
	Bunting		
35	Cape	Rooivlerkstreepkoppie	☐
36	Cinnamon-breasted	Klipstreepkoppie	☐
34	Golden-breasted	Rooirugstreepkoppie	☐
37	Lark-like	Vaalstreepkoppie	☐
	Bustard		
38	Black-bellied	Langbeenkorhaan	☐
31	Denham's	Veldpou	☐
30	Kori	Gompou	☐
	Buttonquail		
06b	Black-rumped	Swartrugkwarteltjie	☐

No.	English	Afrikaans	
205	Kurrichane	Bosveldkwarteltjie	☐
	Buzzard		
152	Jackal	Rooiborsjakkalsvoël	☐
154	Lizard	Akkedisvalk	☐
149	Steppe	Bruinjakkalsvoël	☐
130	European Honey-	Wespedief	☐
	Camaroptera		
657a	Green-backed	Groenrugkwêkwêvoël	☐
657b	Grey-backed	Grysrugkwêkwêvoël	☐
	Canary		
870	Black-throated	Bergkanarie	☐
877	Brimstone	Dikbekkanarie	☐
872	Cape	Kaapse Kanarie	☐
871	Lemon-breasted	Geelborskanarie	☐
869	Yellow-fronted	Geeloogkanarie	☐
	Chat		
594	Arnot's	Bontpiek	☐
589	Familiar	Gewone Spekvreter	☐
593	Mocking Cliff-	Dassievoël	☐
	Cisticola		
666	Cloud	Gevlekte Klopkloppie	☐
678	Croaking	Groottinktinkie	☐
665	Desert	Woestynklopkloppie	☐
677	Levaillant's	Vleitinktinkie	☐
672	Rattling	Bosveldtinktinkie	☐
674	Red-faced	Rooiwangtinktinkie	☐
675a	Rufous-winged	Swartrugtinktinkie	☐
667	Wing-snapping	Kleinste Klopkloppie	☐
664	Zitting	Landeryklopkloppie	☐
	Coot		
228	Red-knobbed	Bleshoender	☐
	Cormorant		
58	Reed	Rietduiker	☐
55	White-breasted	Witborsduiker	☐
	Coucal		
388	Black	Swartvleiloerie	☐
391	Burchell's	Gewone Vleiloerie	☐
	Courser		
303	Bronze-winged	Bronsvlerkdrawwertjie	☐
299	Burchell's	Bloukopdrawwertjie	☐
300	Temminck's	Trekdrawwertjie	☐
302	Three-banded	Driebanddrawwertjie	☐
	Crake		
212	African	Afrikaanse Riethaan	☐
215	Baillon's	Kleinriethaan	☐
213	Black	Swartriethaan	☐
216	Striped	Gestreepte Riethaan	☐

continued on p124

Bird Checklist

	Crane				Eagle		
209	Grey Crowned	Mahem	☐	148	African Fish-	Visarend	✓
	Crombec			137	African Hawk-	Grootjagarend	☐
651	Long-billed	Bosveldstompstert	☐	141	African Crowned	Kroonarend	☐
	Crow			138	Ayres's Hawk-	Kleinjagarend	☐
547	Cape	Swartkraai	☐	136	Booted	Dwergarend	☐
549	House	Huiskraai	☐	143	Black-chested Snake-	Swartborsslangarend	✓
548	Pied	Witborskraai	☐	142	Brown Snake-	Bruinslangarend	☐
	Cuckoo			134	Lesser Spotted	Gevlekte Arend	☐
375	African	Afrikaanse Koekoek	☐	139	Long-crested	Langkuifarend	☐
384	African Emerald	Mooimeisie	☐	140	Martial	Breëkoparend	☐
378	Black	Swartkoekoek	☐	133	Steppe	Steppe-arend	☐
374	Common	Europese Koekoek	☐	132	Tawny	Roofarend	✓
386	Diderick	Diederikkie	☐	131	Verreauxs'	Witkruisarend	☐
380	Great Spotted	Gevlekte Koekoek	☐	135	Wahlberg	Wahlberg-arend	☐
382	Jacobin	Bontnuwejaarsvoël	☐		Egret		
385	Klaas's	Meitjie	☐	71	Cattle	Veereier	☐
381	Levaillant's	Gestreepte Nuwejaarsvoël	☐	66	Great	Grootwitreier	☐
				67	Little	Kleinwitreier	☐
377	Red-chested	Piet-my-vrou	☐	68	Yellow-billed	Geelbekwitreier	☐
383	Thick-billed	Dikbekkoekoek	☐		Eremomela		
	Cuckooshrike			656	Burnt-necked	Bruinkeelbossanger	☐
538	Black	Swartkatakoeroe	☐	655	Green-capped	Donkerwangbossanger	☐
540	Grey	Bloukatakoeroe	☐	653	Yellow-bellied	Geelpensbossanger	☐
539	White-breasted	Witborskatakoeroe	☐		Falcon		
	Darter			180	Amur	Oostelike Rooipootvalk	☐
60	African	Slanghalsvoël	☐	172	Lanner	Edelvalk	☐
	Dove			171	Peregrine	Swerfvalk	☐
353	African Mourning	Rooioogtortelduif	☐	186	Pygmy	Dwergvalk	☐
357	Blue-spotted Wood-	Blouvlekduifie	☐	179	Red-footed	Westelike Rooipootvalk	☐
354	Cape Turtle-	Gewone Tortelduif	☐	178	Red-necked	Rooinekvalk	☐
358	Emerald-spotted Wood-	Groenvlekduifie	☐	175	Sooty	Roetvalk	☐
355	Laughing	Rooiborsduifie	☐		Finch		
360	Lemon	Kaneelduifie	☐	820	Cuckoo	Koekoekvink	☐
356	Namaqua	Namakwaduifie	☐	855	Cut-throat	Bandkeelvink	☐
352	Red-eyed	Grootringduif	✓	856	Red-headed	Rooikopvink	☐
359	Tambourine	Witborsduifie	☐	806	Scaly-feathered	Baardmannetjie	☐
	Drongo				Finchlark		
541	Fork-tailed	Mikstertbyvanger	☐	515	Chestnut-backed	Rooiruglewerik	☐
	Duck				Finfoot		
105	African Black	Swarteend	☐	229	African	Watertrapper	☐
115	Comb	Knobbeleend	☐		Firefinch		
100	Fulvous	Fluiteend	☐	840	African	Kaapse Vuurvinkie	☐
117	Maccoa	Bloubekeend	☐	841	Jameson's	Jamesonse Vuurvinkie	☐
101	White-backed	Witrugeend	☐	842	Red-billed	Rooibekvuurvinkie	☐
99	White-faced	Nonnetjie-eend	☐		Fiscal		
104	Yellow-billed	Geelbekeend	☐	732	Common	Fiskaallaksman	☐
273	Dunlin	Bontstrandloper	☐		Flamingo		
				96	Greater	Grootflamink	☐

Bird Checklist

No.	English	Afrikaans	✓
	Lesser Flufftail	Kleinflamink	□
3	Buff-spotted	Gevlekte Vleikuiken	□
7	Red-chested Flycatcher	Rooiborsvleikuiken	□
)	African Paradise-	Paradysvlieëvanger	□
)	African Dusky	Donkervlieëvanger	□
◀	Ashy	Blougrysvlieëvanger	□
8	Blue-mantled Crested-	Bloukuifvlieëvanger	□
5	Fairy	Feevlieëvanger	□
3	Fiscal	Fiskaalvlieëvanger	□
3	Grey Tit-	Waaierstertvlieëvanger	□
5	Marico	Maricovlieëvanger	□
5	Pale	Muiskleurvlieëvanger	□
4	Southern Black	Swartvlieëvanger	□
9	Spotted	Europese Vlieëvanger	□
	Francolin		
3	Coqui	Swempie	□
9	Crested	Bospatrys	□
1	Shelley's	Laeveldpatrys	□
	Gallinule		
4	Allen's	Kleinkoningriethaan	□
)	Garganey	Somereend	□
	Go-away-bird		
3	Grey	Kwêvoël	✓
	Goose		
4	African Pygmy-	Dwerggans	□
2	Egyptian	Kolgans	✓
6	Spur-winged	Wildemakou	□
	Goshawk		
)	African	Afrikaanse Sperwer	□
3	Dark Chanting	Donkersingvalk	□
4	Gabar	Witkruissperwer (Kleinsingvalk)	□
	Grebe		
	Little	Kleindobbertjie	□
	Greenbul		
2	Sombre	Gewone Willie	□
4	Yellow-bellied	Geelborswillie	□
	Greenshank		
)	Common	Groenpootruiter	□
	Guineafowl		
4	Crested	Kuifkoptarentaal	□
3	Helmeted	Gewone Tarentaal	✓
	Gull		
5	Grey-headed	Gryskopmeeu	□
	Hamerkop	Hamerkop	□
	Harrier		
6	African Marsh-	Afrikaanse Vleivalk	□

No.	English	Afrikaans	✓
166	Montagu's	Blouvleivalk	□
167	Pallid	Witborsvleivalk	□
164	Western Marsh-Harrier-Hawk	Europese Vleivalk	□
169	African Hawk	Kaalwangvalk	□
128	African Cuckoo-Bat Heron	Koekoekvalk Vlermuisvalk	□
129			
69	Black	Swartreier	□
76	Black-crowned Night-	Gewone Nagreier	□
63	Black-headed	Swartkopreier	□
64	Goliath	Reusereier	□
74	Green-backed	Groenrugreier	□
62	Grey	Bloureier	✓
65	Purple	Rooireier	□
75	Rufous-bellied	Rooipensreier	□
72	Squacco	Ralreier	□
77	White-backed Night-Hobby	Witrugnagreier	□
174	African	Afrikaanse Boomvalk	□
173	Eurasian Honeybird	Europese Boomvalk	□
478	Brown-backed Honeyguide	Skerpbekheuningvoël	□
474	Greater	Grootheuningwyser	□
476	Lesser	Kleinheuningwyser	□
475	Scaly-throated Hoopoe	Gevlekte Heuningwyser	□
451	African Hornbill	Hoephoep	□
457	African Grey	Grysneushoringvoël	□
460	Crowned	Gekroonde Neushoringvoël	□
458a	Red-billed	Rooibekneushoringvoël	✓
463	Southern Ground-	Bromvoël	✓
459	Southern Yellow-billed	Geelbek-neushoringvoël	□
455	Trumpeter Hyliota	Gewone Boskraai	□
624	Southern Ibis	Mashonahyliota	□
91	African Sacred	Skoorsteenveër	□
93	Glossy	Glansibis	□
94	Hadeda Indigobird	Hadeda	✓
864	Dusky	Gewone Blouvinkie	□
867	Village	Staalblouvinkie	□
865	Purple	Witpootblouvinkie	□

continued on p126

No.	English	Afrikaans	✓
	Jacana		
240	African	Grootlangtoon	□
241	Lesser	Dwerglangtoon	□
	Jaeger		
307	Parasitic	Arktiese Roofmeeu	□
	Kestrel		
185	Dickinson's	Dickinsonse Grysvalk	□
182	Greater	Grootrooivalk	□
183	Lesser	Kleinrooivalk	□
181	Rock	Kransvalk	□
	Kingfisher		
432	African Pygmy-	Dwergvisvanger	□
435	Brown-hooded	Bruinkopvisvanger	□
429	Giant	Reusevisvanger	□
436	Grey-headed	Gryskopvisvanger	□
430	Half-collared	Blouvisvanger	□
431	Malachite	Kuifkopvisvanger	□
428	Pied	Bontvisvanger	□
437	Striped	Gestreepte Visvanger	□
433	Woodland	Bosveldvisvanger	□
	Kite		
126a	Black	Swartwou	□
127	Black-shouldered	Blouvalk	□
126b	Yellow-billed	Geelbekwou	□
	Korhaan		
237	Red-crested	Boskorhaan	✓
	Lapwing		
260	African Wattled	Lelkiewiet	□
258	Blacksmith	Bontkiewiet	✓
255	Crowned	Kroonkiewiet	✓
256	Senegal	Kleinswartvlerkkiewiet	□
259	White-crowned	Witkopkiewiet	□
	Lark		
505	Dusky	Donkerlewerik	□
497	Fawn-coloured	Vaalbruinlewerik	□
496	Flappet	Laeveldklappertjie	□
493	Monotonous	Bosveldlewerik	□
507	Red-capped	Rooikoplewerik	□
494	Rufous-naped	Rooineklewerik	□
498	Sabota	Sabotalewerik	□
	Longclaw		
728	Yellow-throated	Geelkeelkalkoentjie	□
	Mannikin		
857	Bronze	Gewone Fret	□
858	Red-backed	Rooirugfret	□
	Martin		
534	Banded	Gebande Oewerswael	□
533	Brown-throated	Afrikaanse Oewerswael	□
530	Common House-	Huisswael	□
529	Rock	Kransswael	[
532	Sand	Europese Oewerswael	[
	Moorhen		
226	Common	Grootwaterhoender	[
227	Lesser	Kleinwaterhoender	[
	Mousebird		
426	Red-faced	Rooiwangmuisvoël	[
424	Speckled	Gevlekte Muisvoël	[
681	Neddicky	Neddikkie	[
	Nicator		
575	Eastern	Geelvleknikator	[
	Nightingale		
609	Thrush	Lysternagtegaal	[
	Nightjar		
404	European	Europese Naguil	[
405	Fiery-necked	Afrikaanse Naguil	[
408	Freckled	Donkernaguil	[
410	Pennant-winged	Wimpelvlerknaguil	[
406	Rufous-cheeked	Rooiwangnaguil	[
409	Square-tailed	Laeveldnaguil	[
	Openbill		
87	African	Oopbekooievaar	[
	Oriole		
544	African Golden	Afrikaanse Wielewaal	[
545	Black-headed	Swartkopwielewaal	[
543	Eurasian Golden	Europese Wielewaal	[
170	Osprey	Visvalk	[
	Ostrich		
1	Common	Volstruis	[
	Owl		
393	African Grass-	Grasuil	[
396	African Scops-	Skopsuil	[
394	African Wood-	Bosuil	[
392	Barn	Nonnetjie-uil	[
395	Marsh	Vlei-uil	[
403	Pel's Fishing	Visuil	[
397	Southern White-faced Scops-	Witwanguil	[
401	Spotted Eagle-	Gevlekte Ooruil	[
402	Verreaux's Eagle-	Reuse-ooruil	[
	Owlet		
399	African Barred	Gebande Uil	[
398	Pearl-spotted	Witkoluil	[
	Oxpecker		
772	Red-billed	Rooibekrenostervoël	[
771	Yellow-billed	Geelbekrenostervoël	[
	Parrot		
363	Brown-headed	Bruinkoppapegaai	[
362b	Grey-headed	Savannepapegaai	[

	English	Afrikaans	
4	Meyer's	Bosveldpapegaai	[ ]
	Pelican		
	Great White	Witpelikaan	[ ]
	Pink-backed	Kleinpelikaan	[ ]
	Penduline-Tit		
3	Grey	Gryskapokvoël	[ ]
	Petronia		
5	Yellow-throated	Geelvlekmossie	[ ]
	Pigeon		
4	African Green-	Papegaaiduif	[ ]
9	Speckled	Kransduif	[ ]
	Pipit		
3	Bushveld	Bosveldkoester	[ ]
6	African	Gewone Koester	[ ]
9	Buffy	Vaalkoester	[ ]
7	Long-billed	Nicholsonse Koester	[ ]
8	Plain-backed	Donkerkoester	[ ]
0	Striped	Gestreepte Koester	[ ]
5	Golden	Goudkoester	[ ]
	Pitta		
1	African	Angolapitta	[ ]
	Plover		
2	Caspian	Asiatiese Strandkiewiet	[ ]
7	Chestnut-banded	Rooibandstrandkiewiet	[ ]
5	Common Ringed	Ringnekstrandkiewiet	[ ]
4	Grey	Grysstrandkiewiet	[ ]
3	Kittlitz's	Geelborsstrandkiewiet	[ ]
9	Three-banded	Driebandstrandkiewiet	[ ]
6	White-fronted	Vaalstrandkiewiet	[ ]
	Pochard		
3	Southern	Bruineend	[ ]
	Pratincole		
4	Collared	Rooivlerksprinkaanvoël	[ ]
	Prinia		
5	Black-chested	Swartbandlangstertjie	[ ]
3	Tawny-flanked	Bruinsylangstertjie	[ ]
0	Puffback	Black-backed Sneeubal	[ ]
	Pytilia		
4	Green-winged	Gewone Melba	[ ]
	Quail		[ ]
0	Common	Afrikaanse Kwartel	[ ]
1	Harlequin	Bontkwartel	
	Quailfinch		[ ]
2	African	Gewone Kwartelvinkie	
	Quelea		[ ]
1	Red-billed	Rooibekkwelea	
	Rail		[ ]

No.	English	Afrikaans	
210	African Raven	Grootriethaan	[ ]
550	White-necked Redshank	Withalskraai	[ ]
268	Common Robin	Rooipootruiter	[ ]
606	White-starred Robin-Chat	Witkoljanfrederik	[ ]
601	Cape	Gewone Janfrederik	[ ]
600	Red-capped	Nataljanfrederik	[ ]
599	White-browed	Heuglinse Janfrederik	[ ]
602	White-throated	Witkeeljanfrederik	[ ]
	Roller		[ ]
450	Broad-billed	Geelbektroupant	[ ]
446	European	Europese Troupant	[x]
447	Lilac-breasted	Gewone Troupant	[✓]
449	Purple	Groottroupant	[ ]
448	Racket-tailed	Knopsterttroupant	[ ]
284	Ruff	Kemphaan	[ ]
281	Sanderling	Drietoonstrandloper	
	Sandgrouse		
347	Double-banded	Dubbelbandsandpatrys	[ ]
	Sandpiper		
264	Common	Gewone Ruiter	[ ]
272	Curlew	Krombekstrandloper	[ ]
265	Green	Witgatruiter	[ ]
269	Marsh	Moerasruiter	[ ]
266	Wood	Bosruiter	
	Saw-wing		[ ]
536	Black	Swartsaagvlerkswael	
	Scimitarbill		
454	Common	Swartbekkakelaar	
	Scrub-Robin		
617	Bearded	Baardwipstert	[ ]
616	Brown	Bruinwipstert	[ ]
613	White-browed	Gestreepte Wipstert	[ ]
118	Secretarybird	Sekretarisvoël	
	Seedeater		[ ]
881	Streaky-headed	Streepkopkanarie	
	Shelduck		[ ]
103	South African	Kopereend	
159	Shikra	Gebande Sperwer	
	Shoveler		[ ]
112	Cape	Kaapse Slopeend	
	Shrike		
739	Crimson-breasted	Rooiborslaksman	[ ]
747	Gorgeous Bush-	Konkoit	[ ]
751	Grey-headed Bush-	Spookvoël	[ ]

continued on p128

Bird Checklist

No.	English	Afrikaans		No.	English	Afrikaans
731	Lesser Grey	Gryslaksman	☐	84	Black	Grootswartooievaar
735	Magpie	Langstertlaksman	☑	89	Marabou	Maraboe
750	Olive Bush-	Olyfboslaksman	☐	88	Saddle-billed	Saalbekooievaar
748	Orange-breasted	Oranjeborsboslaksman	☐	83	White	Witooievaar
733	Red-backed	Rooiruglaksman	☐	86	Woolly-necked	Wolnekooievaar
754	Retz's Helmet-	Swarthelmlaksman	☐	90	Yellow-billed	Nimmersat
756	S. White-crowned	Kremetartlaksman	☐		Sugarbird	
753	White-crested Helmet-	Withelmlaksman		774	Gurney's	Rooiborssuikervoël
	Snipe		☐		Sunbird	
286	African	Afrikaanse Snip	☐	792	Amethyst	Swartsuikerbekkie
242	Greater Painted-	Goudsnip		793	Collared	Kortbeksuikerbekkie
	Sparrow		☐	779	Marico	Maricosuikerbekkie
803	Cape	Gewone Mossie	☐	794	Plain-backed	Bloukeelsuikerbekkie
801	House	Huismossie	☐	780	Purple-banded	Purperbandsuikerbekkie
804	Southern Grey-headed	Gryskopmossie		791	Scarlet-chested	Rooiborssuikerbekkie
	Sparrowhawk		☐	786	Variable	Geelpenssuikerbekkie
158	Black	Swartsperwer	☐	787	White-bellied	Witpenssuikerbekkie
157	Little	Kleinsperwer	☐		Swallow	
156	Ovambo	Ovambosperwer		518	Barn	Europese Swael
	Spinetail		☐	526	Greater Striped	Grootstreepswael
423	Böhm's	Witpensstekelstert	☐	531	Grey-rumped	Gryskruisswael
422	Mottled	Gevlekte Stekelstert	☐	527	Lesser Striped	Kleinstreepswael
	Spoonbill		☐	525	Mosque	Moskeeswael
95	African	Lepelaar	☑	523	Pearl-breasted	Pêrelborsswael
	Spurfowl		☐	524	Red-breasted	Rooiborsswael
196	Natal	Natalse Fisant	☐	520	White-throated	Witkeelswael
198	Red-necked	Rooikeelfisant	☑	522	Wire-tailed	Draadstertswael
199	Swainson's	Bosveldfisant			Swamphen	
	Starling			223	African Purple	Grootkoningriethaan
768	Black-bellied	Swartpensglans-	☐		Swift	
		spreeu	☐	421	African Palm-	Palmwindswael
762	Burchell's	Grootglansspreeu	☐	412	African Black	Swartwindswael
764	Cape Glossy	Kleinglansspreeu	☑	418	Alpine	Witpenswindswael
765	Greater Blue-eared	Groot-	☐	411	Common	Europese Windswael
		blouoorglansspreeu	☐	416	Horus	Horuswindswael
763	Meves's	Langstertglansspreeu		417	Little	Kleinwindswael
766	Miombo Blue-eared	Klein-		415	White-rumped	Witkruiswindswael
		blouoorglansspreeu	☐		Tchagra	
769	Red-winged	Rooivlerkspreeu	☐	744	Black-crowned	Swartkroontjagra
761	Violet-backed	Witborsspreeu	☐	743	Brown-crowned	Rooivlerktjagra
760	Wattled	Lelspreeu			Teal	
	Stilt		☐	106	Cape	Teeleend
295	Black-winged	Rooipootelsie	☐	107	Hottentot	Gevlekte Eend
	Stint		☐	108	Red-billed	Rooibekeend
274	Little	Kleinstrandloper			Tern	
	Stonechat		☐	332	Sooty	Roetseeswael
596	African	Gewone Bontrokkie	☐	338	Whiskered	Witbaardmeerswael
	Stork		☐	339	White-winged	Witvlerkmeerswael
85	Abdim's	Kleinswartooievaar	☐		Thick-knee	

No.	English	Afrikaans	☐
'7	Spotted	Gewone Dikkop	☐
'8	Water Thrush	Waterdikkop	☐
'3	Collared Palm-	Palmmôrelyster	☐
'0	Groundscraper	Gevlekte Lyster	☐
'6	Kurrichane Tinkerbird	Rooibeklyster	☐
'0	Yellow-fronted	Geelblestinker	☐
'1	Yellow-rumped Tit	Swartblestinker	☐
'2	Ashy	Akasiagrysmees	☐
'4	Southern Tit-Babbler	Gewone Swartmees	☐
'1	Chestnut-vented Trogon	Bosveldtjeritik	☐
'7	Narina Turaco	Bosloerie	
'1	Purple-crested Turnstone	Bloukuifloerie	☐
'2	Ruddy Twinspot	Steenloper	☐
'8	Pink-throated	Rooskeelkolpensie	☐
'9	Red-throated	Rooikeelkolpensie	☐
'5	Green Vulture	Groenkolpensie	☐
'2	Cape	Kransaasvoël	☐
'0	Egyptian	Egiptiese Aasvoël	☐
'1	Hooded	Monnikaasvoël	☐
'4	Lappet-faced	Swartaasvoël	☐
'7	Palm-nut	Witaasvoël	☐
'3	White-backed	Witrugaasvoël	☑
'5	White-headed Wagtail	Witkopaasvoël	☐
1	African Pied	Bontkwikkie	☐
3	Cape	Gewone Kwikkie	☐
2	Mountain	Bergkwikkie	☐
4	Yellow Warbler	Geelkwikkie	☐
'1	African Reed-	Kleinrietsanger	☐
'2	Broad-tailed	Breëstertsanger	☐
'7	Dark-capped Yellow	Geelsanger	☐
'9	Garden	Tuinsanger	☐
'8	Great Reed-	Grootrietsanger	☐
'5	Icterine	Spotsanger	☑
'5	Lesser Swamp-	Kaapse Rietsanger	☐
'8	Little Rush-	Kaapse Vleisanger	☐
'3	Marsh	Europese Rietsanger	☐
'6	Olive-tree	Olyfboomsanger	☐
'7	River	Sprinkaansanger	☐

No.	English	Afrikaans	☐
634	Sedge	Europese Vleisanger	☐
659	Stierling's Wren-	Stierlingse Sanger	☐
643	Willow Wattle-eye	Hofsanger	☐
705	Black-throated Waxbill	Beloogbosbontrokkie	☐
844	Blue	Gewone Blousysie	☐
846	Common	Rooibeksysie	☐
845	Violet-eared	Koningblousysie	☐
848	Grey	Gryssysie	☐
854	Orange-breasted	Rooiassie	☐
850	Swee Weaver	Suidelike Swie	☐
816	Golden	Goudwewer	☐
815	Lesser Masked-	Kleingeelvink	☐
798	Red-billed Buffalo-	Buffelwewer	☐
814	Southern Masked-	Swartkeelgeelvink	☐
810	Spectacled	Brilwewer	☐
811	Village	Bontrugwewer	☐
799	White-browed Sparrow	Koringvoël	☐
817	Yellow	Geelwewer	☐
819	Red-headed	Rooikopwewer	☐
807	Thick-billed Wheatear	Dikbekwewer	☐
587	Capped	Hoëveldskaapwagter	☐
586	Mountain	Bergwagter	☐
585	Northern Whimbrel	Europese Skaapwagter	☐
290	Common White-eye	Kleinwulp	☐
797	African Yellow	Geelglasogie	☐
796a	Cape Whydah	Kaapse Glasogie	☐
862	Long-tailed Paradise-	Gewone Paradysvink	☐
860	Pin-tailed	Koningrooibekkie	☐
861	Shaft-tailed Widowbird	Pylstertrooibekkie	☐
828	Fan-tailed	Kortstertflap	☐
831	Red-collared	Rooikeelflap	☐
829	White-winged Wood-Hoopoe	Witvlerkflap	☐
452	Green Woodpecker	Rooibekkakelaar	☐
487	Bearded	Baardspeg	☐
481	Bennett's	Bennettse Speg	☐
486	Cardinal	Kardinaalspeg	☐
483	Golden-tailed Wryneck	Goudstertspeg	☐
489	Red-throated	Draaihals	

129

Acknowledgements

The publisher would like to thank the following people for their contribution to this book:

Reneé Ferreira for her technical advice and for editing the manuscript.

Dr Andrew Deacon of SANParks for his advice on the reptiles and amphibians of the Greater Kruger Park.

Karen Pretorius of NuDog Design for her patience and useful ideas.

All the wildlife photographers who made available their material.

Tudor Photographic for supporting our photographers with Sigma equipment.

BIBLIOGRAPHY

Branch, B. 1998. **Field guide to snakes and other reptiles of Southern Africa.** Struik Publishers, Cape Town.

Branch, B. 2000. **Everyone's guide to snakes, other reptiles & amphibians of Southern Africa.** Struik Publishers, Cape Town.

Bronner, G. N., Hoffmann, M., Taylor, P. J., Chimamba, C. T., Best, P. B., Matthee, C. A. & Robinson, T. J. 2003. **A revised systematic checklist of the extant mammals of the southern African subregion.** Durban Museum, Durban.

Cillié, B. & Oberprieler, U. B. 1999. **Pocket-guide to Southern African birds.** Sunbird Publishing, Cape Town.

Cillié, B. 2003. **Pocket-Photoguide to Southern African mammals.** Sunbird Publishing, Cape Town.

Cillié, B. 2004. **The mammal guide of Southern Africa.** Briza Publications, Pretoria.

Ginn, P. J., McIlleron, D. G., Milstein, P le S. 1989. **The complete book of Southern African birds.** Struik Winchester, Cape Town.

Harrison, J. A., Allen, D. G., Underhill, L. G., Herremans, M., Tree, A. J., Parker, V. & Brown, C. J (eds). 1997. **The atlas of Southern African birds: Vol. 1 & 2.** BirdLife South Africa. Johannesburg.

Labuschagne, R. J. 1958. **60 Jaar Krugerwildtuin.** National Parks Board of South Africa, Pretoria.

Oberprieler, U. B. & Cillié, B. 2002. **Raptor identification guide for Southern Africa.** Rollerbird Press, Johannesburg.

Pienaar, U. de V., Passmore, N. I. & Carruthers, V. C. 1976. **The frogs of the Kruger National Park.** National Parks Board of South Africa, Pretoria.

Pienaar, U. de V. 1966. **The reptiles of the Kruger National Park.** National Parks Board of South Africa, Pretoria.

Sinclair, I., Hockey, P. & Tarboton, W. 2003. **Sasol birds of Southern Africa.** Struik Publishers, Cape Town.

Skinner, J. D. & Chimimba, C. T. 2005. **The mammals of the Southern African subregion.** Cambridge University Press, Cambridge.

Quick index

MAMMALS

Aardvark	24
Aardwolf	13
Baboon	28
Bat	31
Buffalo	17
Bushbaby	27
Bushbuck	20
Bushpig	24
Canerat	32
Caracal	16
Cheetah	15
Civet	11
Dassie	31
Dormouse	28
Duiker	22
Eland	19
Elephant	26
Galago	27
Genet	11
Gerbil	32
Giraffe	25
Grysbok	23
Hare	30
Hartebeest	18
Hippopotamus	25
Honey Badger	12
Hyaena	13
Hyrax	31
Impala	18
Jackal	14
Klipspringer	22
Kudu	20
Leopard	15
Lion	15
Mongoose	9, 10
Monkey	28
Mouse	32
Nyala	20
Otter	12
Polecat	12
Porcupine	30
Rat	31
Reedbuck	21
Rhinoceros	26
Roan Antelope	19
Sable Antelope	19
Serval	16

Springhare	30
Squirrel	29
Steenbok	23
Suni	23
Tsessebe	18
Waterbuck	21
Warthog	24
Wildebeest	17
Wild Cat	16
Wild Dog	14
Zebra	25

BIRDS

Apalis	99
Babbler	88
Barbet	64, 65
Bateleur	58
Batis	91
Bee-eater	73, 74
Bishop	105
Boubou	83
Buffalo-Weaver	103
Bulbul	92
Bunting	107
Bustard	44
Buzzard	59
Camaroptera	99
Canary	107
Chat	91
Cisticola	100
Cliff-chat	91
Cormorant	37
Coucal	79
Courser	50
Crake	45
Crombec	98
Crow	79
Cuckoo	85, 86
Darter	37
Dove	104
Drongo	87
Duck	36
Eagle	56, 57, 58
Eagle-Owl	54
Egret	40
Finch	105
Firefinch	105
Fish-Eagle	58

Flycatcher	87, 95
Francolin	53
Go-away-bird	63
Goose	36
Goshawk	59
Grebe	35
Greenbul	92
Green-Pigeon	63
Greenshank	49
Guineafowl	51
Hamerkop	38
Harrier-Hawk	60
Heron	39, 40
Hoopoe	72
Hornbill	70, 71
Ibis	43
Jacana	45
Kingfisher	66, 67, 68
Kite	57, 70
Korhaan	44
Lark	94
Lapwing	47
Longclaw	93
Mannikin	106
Moorhen	35
Mousebird	62
Neddicky	100
Nightjar	76
Oriole	88
Ostrich	38
Owl	54, 55
Oxpecker	95
Parrot	64
Petronia	104
Pipit	93
Plover	46
Prinia	99
Ptylia	106
Puffback	82
Quelea	106
Robin-Chat	89
Roller	80, 81
Ruff	49
Sandgrouse	52
Sandpiper	48, 49
Scops-Owl	55
Scrub-Robin	90
Secretarybird	58
Shrike	81, 82, 84

Snake-Eagle	56, 57
Sparrow	101
Spoonbill	43
Spurfowl	52
Starling	96, 97
Stilt	48
Stork	41, 42
Sunbird	74, 75
Swallow	77, 78
Swift	78
Tchagra	83
Thick-knee	50
Thrush	88, 90
Tinkerbird	65
Tit	87
Tit-babbler	100
Turaco	63
Vulture	60, 61
Wagtail	93
Waxbill	104
Weaver	102, 103
White-eye	98
Whydah	108
Widowbird	108
Wood-hoopoe	72
Woodpecker	68, 69

REPTILES

Adder	113
Agama	116
Chameleon	117
Cobra	113
Crocodile	116
Gecko	116
Lizard	115
Mamba	113
Monitor	114
Python	114
Skink	115
Snake	112
Terrapin	117
Tortoise	117

AMPHIBIANS

Frog	119, 120
Toad	118

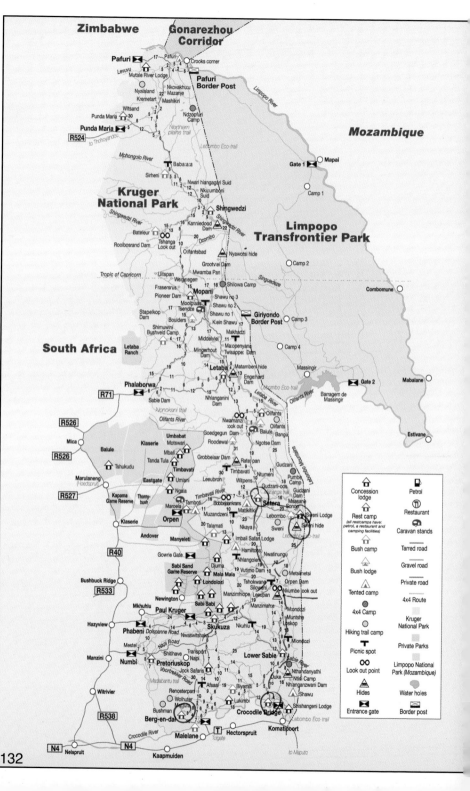